{The New}

NEW SOUTHERN BASICS

{ *The New* }

NEW
SOUTHERN
BASICS

TRADITIONAL

SOUTHERN FOOD

FOR TODAY

MARTHA STAMPS

A CUMBERLAND HOUSE HEARTHSIDE BOOK
CUMBERLAND HOUSE
NASHVILLE, TENNESSEE

THE NEW NEW SOUTHERN BASICS
PUBLISHED BY CUMBERLAND HOUSE PUBLISHING
431 Harding Industrial Drive
Nashville, Tennessee 37211

Cover by Becky Brawner/Unlikely Suburban Design
Text Design by Julie Pitkin
Illustrations by JulesRulesDesign

Library of Congress Cataloging-in-Publication Data

Stamps, Martha Phelps, 1961–
  New Southern basics : traditional Southern food for today / Martha Phelps Stamps.
      p. cm. — (A Cumberland House hearthside book)
  Includes index.
  ISBN-13 978-1-58182-432-2 (alk. paper)
  1. Cookery, American—Southern style. I. Title. II. Series.

TX715.2.S68S8 2007
641.5975—dc22

                                        2007029557

Printed in Canada
1 2 3 4 5 6 7 — 11 10 09 08 07

To Catherine Couch
and my children,
Moria, Sadie, and John Mark.

CONTENTS

SO WHY A *NEW NEW*?

I wanted to compile a second edition to *The New Southern Basics* because the original book's function remains relevant today. These are recipes that really work in any modern home. Things your family will love, your friends will love, your boss' picky kids will love. They work in a home—not just a fancy restaurant. The directions are clear, and don't require any special skills or knowledge. The ingredients are ones you probably already have, or at least that you can find without driving all over town. That's the "basic" part.

I write about southern food because that's where I live, it's who I am. The South is home base for my culinary odyssey. I began this collection because I felt that the south was maligned—that most people, southerners included, had no idea of the rich heritage behind their everyday food, or that everyday southern food could be something quite extraordinary. We frequently fail to recognize the treasures in front of our faces – or in mouths, for that matter.

As a southern chef, I'm always approached by folks who want to know the low-down on cooking southern food. Southerners who want to cook like their mom or dad, transplants to the south who just need a place to start, and transplants from the south who want a taste of home.

Ten more years of living and cooking has yielded ten more years of recipes. As soon as the "old" *The New Southern Basics* was released, I thought of so many things that I wished I had included. Ten years has also expanded my idea of what "southern" means. My children know a south spiced with Hispanic, Middle Eastern, and Asian tastes. While I want to preserve the foods particular to my grandmother's south, I celebrate these new flavors, as well.

The New Southern Basics is my first book, and my favorite still, today. *The New New* is expanded, corrected in spots, tweaked and brought up to date...for now, at least.

INTRODUCTION

In 1997, I noted a change in the culinary realm, "a culinary Renaissance, if you will." Ten years later, I'm happy to report that Renaissance is still in full swing. The food channel, celebrity chefs, the growth of culinary schools and movements such as Slow Food all point to our still growing passion for food.

When I first wrote *The New Southern Basics* I believed our culture was yearning for simpler times, family values, a slower rhythm to our hectic lives. Ironically, as technology has continued to increase and schedules become even more overloaded, an undercurrent has continued to grow—one desirous of simple pleasures and basic delight. Those pleasures come to me through a connection to this living Earth—the land, the animals, the people.

What does this have to do with food, you may be asking. Everything, my friend. The land supports us all. A healthy Earth gives forth food which nurtures both animals and man. Cultivation a basic tenent of all of civilization. Here in the south we remained more closely connected to our agrarian roots for a longer time than in the industrialized north. An agrarian life is one ruled by the rhythms of nature. Waxing and waning moons, sunrise and sunset, the change of the seasons, the cycle of life and death. I would suggest that modern life is far removed from that natural beat. Most vegetables are in season whenever we want—we have no sense of anticipation for the first peach of the season, for spring chickens, or autumn apples. We get what we want when we want it. No wonder our children are spoiled! So are we.

Children have no idea where a hot dog or mcnugget comes from. It all just magically appears—from the freezer, the grocery store, the drive-through window.

And what do we do when we're eating? Watching tv, playing video games, driving in our cars to one more activity. My point is, we're not eating together, as families, as friends. We know more intimate details about celebrities' lives than we do about our neighbors, our co-workers, our kids. I say all of this in self-incrimination as well. I'm as caught up in this frantic race for a life well-lived as anyone. But in the back of my mind, a quiet, yet annoyingly insistent voice urges me to slow it down.

This simple suggestion could play a very large role in our lives – certainly in what we eat, how we cook, with whom we share a meal.

Sharing a meal—this common thread runs through so many stories—a sacred rite of humanity. We can make little choices each day—to buy local, to cook from scratch, to turn off the dang t.v. Little choices can make big changes, Sometimes we don't know how far we've come until we look back on where we were. We have come a long way. It might take a while to get back.

{ *The New* }

NEW
SOUTHERN
BASICS

{ Chapter 1 }

THE PANTRY

The Southern pantry was much more than a dark room off to the side of the kitchen. The pantry served as a vital organ in that kitchen. It was a year round flavor connection to summer, the storehouse of fruits and vegetables picked at their peak. Furthermore, pantry pickles and relishes provided a great deal of the flavor in many meals. Lightly seasoned roasts, potatoes, sandwiches, and stews all came alive with the vinegar and spices from the relish tray. A dining room table would have a special relish tray of silver or cut glass with three to five compartments for holding chow chow, bread and butter pickles, and maybe chutney or cranberry sauce. The kitchen table played host to three to five glass jars, their lids removed and a spoon unceremoniously stuck inside. However they were served, pickles and preserves were there at almost every meal, and a bottle of hot sauce, too.

But what we really lost when we stopped "putting up" these things ourselves was a great deal more than flavor. We're missing out on the fellowship and ritual of folks gathered together in the kitchen, working around the table, gossiping, laughing, and sharing each others' lives as well as their recipes. Sure, there are some pretty good pickles and jellies at the grocery store. But those clerks in that store aren't going to tell you what to do about your boyfriend or how to stop your baby's ear aches or why your roses won't bloom. A big chore like preserving is easier when it's a group effort. You'll get the job done quicker, and every time you taste those peach preserves, you can also taste the smiles and jokes of someone you love.

CHILI SAUCE

A sweet and sour relish, used on meats and vegetables alike.

{ MAKES 3 QUARTS. }

5	pounds ripe tomatoes
2	sticks cinnamon
1	teaspoons whole cloves
1	tablespoons black peppercorns
1	pounds green bell peppers
½	pound brown sugar
1	heads garlic, peeled and minced
2½	pounds onions, chopped fine
½	cup grated fresh horseradish
2	teaspoons salt

Bring a large pot of water to a simmer. Prepare a large bowl with ice water. Core the tomatoes and blanch in batches in simmering water for about 1 minute, until the skin pulls away easily. Remove from the pot and plunge into the ice water. When cool, remove from the ice water, peel, squeezing out as many seeds as you can without making yourself crazy. Place the tomatoes in a heavy pot and cook down for 1 hour, stirring occasionally.

While the tomatoes are cooking, use a coffee grinder or a mortar and pestle to grind the cinnamon sticks, cloves, and peppercorns very fine. Add along with the other ingredients and cook for 2 hours. Taste for seasoning. Pour into sterile jars and process in a water bath to keep indefinitely, or cover and refrigerate for up to 2 weeks.

TOMATO KETCHUP

This is really marvelous. French fries will never be the same!

{ MAKES 4 TO 5 QUARTS. }

5	pounds ripe tomatoes
2	onions, chopped
6	cloves garlic, minced
3	cups vinegar
½	cup horseradish

 2 bell peppers, chopped

 2 teaspoons dry mustard

1½ teaspoons celery seed

 1 tablespoon black pepper

 1 teaspoons red pepper

 ¼ cup salt

*B*lanch the tomatoes in simmering water for about 30 seconds. Place in ice water. Peel and roughly chop. Boil until thick and soft.

 Strain through a sieve. There should be 1 gallon of pulp. Place back in the pot and add the remaining ingredients. Boil slowly 1 hour or more until thick, stirring frequently to prevent burning. Bottle and seal while still hot.

CHOW CHOW

A great all around condiment to add flavor to lightly seasoned foods.

{ MAKES ABOUT 7 PINTS. }

 6 pounds cabbage

 6 green tomatoes

 2 large yellow onions

 3 cayenne peppers

 ½ cup salt

 ½ pound sugar

 1 quart vinegar

 1 tablespoon turmeric

 1 tablespoon ground ginger

 ½ tablespoon celery seed

 ½ tablespoon ground cloves

 ½ tablespoon ground cinnamon

*P*ut the vegetables through a food grinder or chop in a food processor. Stir in the salt. Place in a colander lined with a cheese-cloth and let drip for 2 hours.

 Add the sugar, vinegar, turmeric, ginger, celery seed, cloves, and cinnamon. Place in a heavy pot and boil together for 20 minutes. Seal in sterile jars.

WATERMELON PICKLE

Sweet and crispy.

{ MAKES ABOUT 12 PINTS. }

    Rind of 1 large watermelon
    Water
    Salt
1   ounce cinnamon sticks
1   teaspoon whole cloves
2   quarts white vinegar
1½ pounds light brown sugar

Peel the watermelon rind, cut in ½-inch thick cubes, and place in a large ceramic bowl. Make a brine of salt and water that is strong enough to float an egg (1 gallon water to ½ cup salt). Pour over the rind; let stand overnight.

Drain, place in a non-reactive pot, and cover with cold water. Bring to a boil and boil the rind about 30 minutes until tender. Drain and set aside.

Boil the spices with the vinegar and sugar. Add the melon and cook until it is clear, about 30 minutes. Pack in sterile jars and process in a water bath.

CABBAGE PICKLE

I eat this right out of the jar. It's in between cole slaw and sauerkraut. Yummy with grilled sausages.

{ MAKES ABOUT 12 PINTS. }

3   quarts water
¾   pound salt
7   pounds shredded cabbage
2   pounds sliced onion
6   banana peppers, cut in ½-inch slices
2   quarts white vinegar

Boil the water with the salt and pour over the cabbage. Cover and let stand overnight.

Drain the cabbage and squeeze as dry as possible. Place the cabbage, onion, and peppers in a pot and pour the vinegar over. Stir and cook for 45 minutes.

Pack in jars and process in a water bath to can indefinitely, or keep covered in the refrigerator for several weeks.

BREAD AND BUTTER PICKLES

The only sweet cucumber pickle I like. The garlic makes it.

{ MAKES ABOUT 6 PINTS. }

2	dozen cucumbers
	Peeled cloves from 1 head garlic
⅔	quart white vinegar
⅓	quart water
1	cup sugar
1½	tablespoons whole mustard seed
1	tablespoon turmeric
1	tablespoon celery seed
	Few cinnamon sticks
1	teaspoon whole cloves
1	teaspoon ground allspice

Slice the cucumbers and sprinkle lightly with salt. Allow to stand overnight.

Drain in the morning. Boil together the garlic, vinegar, water, and sugar with the spices. Add the cucumbers and boil about 20 minutes until tender.

Place in sterilized jars and seal. Process in a water bath.

DILL PICKLES

A classic, and very pretty with the dill sprigs.

{ MAKES 2 1-QUART JARS. }

	About 18 to 20 smallest cucumbers, finger size
2	large sprigs dill with seeds
2	small bay leaves
6	fresh cayenne peppers
1	quart water
1	quart white vinegar

Clean the cucumbers and pack in sterile jars, along with 1 sprig of dill, 1 bay leaf, and 3 cayenne peppers per jar. Boil the water with the vinegar and pour over the cucumber. Seal in a hot water bath.

MUSTARD PICKLE

Try this with roasted meats like lamb or pork loin.

{ MAKES ABOUT 12 PINTS. }

4 pints water
1 pint salt

1 quart chopped green tomatoes (4 medium tomatoes)
1 quart chopped onion (2 onions)
1 cauliflower, divided into florets
4 green bell peppers, diced
4 red bell peppers, diced
4 stalks celery, diced
1 cup all-purpose flour
6 tablespoons dry mustard
1 tablespoon turmeric
1 tablespoon celery seed
1 cup sugar
6 cups white vinegar
1 quart ¼-inch thick cucumber slices (about 4 cucumbers)

Boil the water with the salt to make a brine and pour over the tomatoes, onion, cauliflower, bell peppers, and celery. Let stand for 24 hours.

Drain and place in a heavy pot. Cover with cold water and bring to a boil. Drain immediately.

Mix the flour, dry mustard, turmeric, celery seed, and sugar together and whisk in the vinegar to make 2 quarts. Place the drained vegetables back in the pot with the cucumber and pour the dressing over. Place on low heat and, stirring frequently, bring to a slight boil. Taste to adjust the seasoning. Pack in jars and process in a water bath.

HOT PEPPER VINEGAR

A bottle of this is obligatory on most Southern tables. For beans and greens, this adds zip to your individual taste.

{ MAKES ABOUT 5 CUPS. }

1   quart distilled white vinegar
1   dozen fresh cayenne peppers
6   peeled garlic cloves
3   tablespoons brown sugar

Mix all of the ingredients, and store in a sealed container.

HOT PEPPER JELLY

Sometime in the seventies (or was it the eighties?) hot pepper jelly was relegated to adorning a block of cream cheese for an instant appetizer. While the aforementioned is indeed tasty, hot pepper jelly can do so much more! We use it to accompany bite–sized chicken croquettes, or atop mini corn cakes with a little dollop of sour cream. Think of the possibilities in your repertoire—this tasty concoction deserves more than cream cheese!

{ MAKES 5 HALF-PINTS. }

½   cup jalapeño peppers, seeded, stemmed, and coarsely chopped
1½   cups cranberry juice cocktail
1   cup vinegar
5   cups sugar
1   foil pouch liquid fruit pectin

In a medium saucepan combine the peppers, cranberry juice, and vinegar. Bring to boiling; reduce the heat. Cover and simmer for about 10 minutes.

In a 4-quart pot combine the pepper mixture and sugar. Bring to a full rolling boil over high heat, stirring constantly. Stir in the pectin. Return to a full rolling boil; boil for 1 minute, stirring constantly. Remove the pan from the heat.

Skim off the foam with a metal spoon. Pour into hot, sterilized half-pint jars and seal with sterilized lids. Process in a hot water bath for 10 minutes.

SPICED PEACHES

These are so welcome on the dinner table in the dead of winter, and year round, of course.

{ MAKES ABOUT 8 PINTS. }

1   tablespoon allspice
2   sticks cinnamon
1   teaspoon whole cloves
1   teaspoon celery seed
1   tablespoon mace
1   quart vinegar
2   pounds sugar
7   pounds peaches, slightly underripe

Tie the spices in cheesecloth and cook for 15 minutes with the vinegar and sugar to make a syrup.

Bring a large pot of water to a slow boil and blanch the peaches for about 1 minute, until the peel pulls away. Remove from the pot and drop in ice water. Peel. Cook the peeled peaches a few at a time in the syrup, until they are easily pierced. As the peaches are cooked, split and remove the pit and spread them out on platters until they all are done.

Cook the syrup down until fairly thick and remove the spices. Pack the peaches in sterile jars, pour the syrup over, and process in a water bath.

PEACH JAM

Summertime in a jar.

{ MAKES ABOUT 4 HALF-PINTS. }

2½   pounds peaches
½   cup water
1   pound sugar
1   stick cinnamon

Bring a pot of water to boil and drop in the peaches. Cook for 1 to 2 minutes, until the skins slip off. Cut the peaches in 1-inch pieces. Place in a non-reactive saucepan with ½ cup of water and bring to a boil. Boil for 10 minutes.

Add the sugar and cinnamon and boil for 20 minutes, stirring occasionally, until the syrup is thickened and a candy thermometer registers at least 216°. Pour while hot into jars and seal.

APPLE BUTTER

Apple butter has an intense flavor, best accentuated with just a little spice. We spread apple butter on a sandwich with smoked turkey and Cheddar. No fat grams makes apple butter a healthy choice, too!

{ MAKES A LITTLE MORE THAN 3 PINTS. }

4   pounds Granny Smith apples, cored and quartered
1   cup apple cider vinegar
2   cups water
4   cups sugar (approximately)
    Salt
2   teaspoons cinnamon
½   teaspoon ginger
¼   teaspoon allspice
    Zest and juice of 1 lemon

Place the unpeeled apple quarters in a large, heavy bottomed pot. Add the vinegar and water, cover, and bring to a boil.

Reduce the heat to simmer and cook until the apples are soft, about 20 minutes. Remove from the heat.

Purée the apple mixture in batches in the food processor. Measure the purée, and add ½ cup of sugar for each cup of apple purée. Stir to dissolve the sugar. Add the salt, cinnamon, ginger, allspice, lemon zest, and juice. Taste and adjust seasonings if necessary.

Cook uncovered in a heavy bottomed pot on medium low heat, stirring frequently. Cook until thick and smooth (about 1 hour and 30 minutes).

Pour into hot, sterilized jars and seal in a hot water bath.

RHUBARB JAM

This is truly very pretty, with the lemon slices, and has a nice tart taste.

{ MAKES ABOUT 8 PINTS. }

6   pounds rhubarb, cut in 1-inch pieces
6   lemons, sliced thin, seeds removed
6   pounds sugar

*P*lace the rhubarb and lemon in a nonreactive bowl and pour the sugar over. Let stand for 24 hours.

   Place in a nonreactive pot and boil for 45 minutes, stirring gently to avoid breaking up the fruit. There should be pieces of fruit and lemon in the finished jam. After 45 minutes, pack in sterile jars and process in a water bath.

APRICOT SUNSHINE JAM

I brought this recipe home from Sunday school when I was a little girl. Recently I wrote a little article about making the jam with my mother—about what an impression our accomplishment had made upon me. Mama has saved an incredible collection of recipes over the years. When she read what I'd written, she starting to dig, and came up with the original text, cut from a Church elementary school paper, complete with sixties–style graphics. The author is Myra B. McKean. I framed the text and made the jam with Sadie and a Brownie friend and her mother. We were all amply impressed. Thank you Myra, wherever you are.

"Cook one pound of dried apricots until tender. * These may be ground with a coarse knife or chopped or left whole and cut up somewhat after being cooked.
Add one small can* of crushed pineapple and as much sugar as there is of the fruit. Boil until thickened. Dip into sterilized, warm glasses. Seal with paraffin."

I added about 1 cup of water when I cooked the apricots, and I puréed them in the food processor after they were soft. It will keep covered in the fridge for up to a month, even without the seal.

BLACKBERRY JAM

Pristine and lip smacking good.

{ MAKES ABOUT 4 HALF-PINTS. }

1	quart blackberries
¼	cup water
4	cups sugar

*R*inse and drain the blackberries. Mash slightly. Place in a saucepan with the water. Bring to a boil and cook for 5 minutes until soft. Add the sugar, stir, and heat to 218°, stirring occasionally. Pour while hot into 4 sterile half-pint jars. Seal and process in a water bath.

PEACH GINGER CHUTNEY

Chutney's become a real standard for me, though there's nothing "standard" about the exotic flavoring mix. We vary the fruit with the season and the seasoning with our mood. The bright flavors of fresh peach and ginger complement any meat just off the summer grill.

{ MAKES ABOUT 12 HALF-PINTS. }

3	quarts roughly chopped, peeled, fresh, almost-ripe peaches (about 9)
1	red onion chopped
2	ounces ginger, peeled, finely chopped
½	box golden raisins
1	cup firmly packed brown sugar
1	cup cider vinegar
1	tablespoon red pepper flakes
2	tablespoons salt
2	tablespoons coriander seed
1	tablespoon fresh garlic
4	cinnamon sticks

*P*lace everything in a heavy bottomed pan and bring to a boil. Stir, reduce the to simmer, and cook for about 30 minutes, until the peaches are tender and the sauce a thick, syrupy consistency. Process in hot, sterilized jars in a hot water bath for 10 minutes, or keep covered and refrigerated for up to 1 month

PEAR AND GINGER CONSERVE

Delicious on toast. This is nice with ham, as well.

{ MAKES ABOUT 10 PINTS. }

8   pounds pear slices (about 10 pounds whole pears)
½   pound candied ginger, finely minced
8   pounds sugar
4   lemons, sliced in thin circles and seeded

Place the pears, ginger, and sugar in a nonreactive saucepan and boil slowly for 1 hour.

While that is cooking, place the lemons in a small nonreactive saucepan, cover with water, and boil for 30 minutes.

Drain the lemon slices and add to the pears. Boil for 30 more minutes. Pour into sterile jars while hot and seal in a water bath.

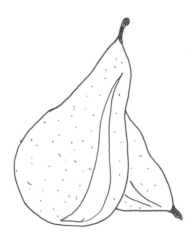

{ Chapter 2 }

SNACKS

Snacks at my grandmother's house were never inconsequential. No bags of Doritoes or cans of dip. Snacks, like the rest of the family's sustenance, were thoughtfully prepared, composed even. While a snack might be casual, it was never mundane. This deliberate essence of snacking had two very positive results. First of all, there was much less compulsive eating. No microwave popcorn to blindly cram into our mouths with our greasy little fists. In fact popcorn itself was a much anticipated treat. On rainy afternoons after school, it could be made on top of the stove in a big pot with a little oil. Remember testing to see how hot the oil was? Grandmama instructed me to use three kernels—no less and no more. Great anticipation and much excitement when you heard the kernels zing, zing, zing against the aluminum lid. The alternate festive option was wire popcorn baskets cooked over an open fire. Campfire popcorn was one of the trappings of a truly exceptional event, a hay ride or possibly an outdoor overnight.

Most snacks were entered into with even greater purpose. Open-face sandwiches were made on white bread rolled out very thin, spread with garlicky homemade mayonnaise and cut out in the perfect size circle to fit the chosen tomato or cucumber slice. A dash of salt and paprika, a crank of the pepper grinder, a garnish of parsley or watercress. Lay these on a silver tray with a doily underneath and carry them to the side porch where folks are enjoying homemade lemonade in tall glasses with thin circles of lemon and sprigs of mint floating on top. That's the way to snack. Listen to bees buzz in the wisteria or maybe the soft thwack of the neighbor's push lawn mower. Have a sandwich and pass the tray. Fall asleep with your head in Mama's lap while the grown-ups talk politics. These were Sunday afternoons at Grandmama's.

The end result of this celebratory snacking is an obvious one. The snacks taste marvelous, to die for. Of course you must take as much time to savor them as it takes to make them. The tomatoes should be slightly warm from the garden. The herbs are best picked just outside the kitchen door. Only make as many sandwiches as you need, for they won't keep well for long. Of course, however many you make will get eaten quickly enough.

COLD CUCUMBER SANDWICHES

{ MAKES ABOUT 18 SMALL SANDWICHES. }

1 fresh cucumber (local, if possible)
½ cup white wine vinegar
1 teaspoon sugar
6 slices white or whole wheat bread, figuring three circles to a bread slice
¼ cup Mayonnaise (see page 29)
   Salt and white pepper
   Fresh dill sprigs

Core the cucumber with the tines of a fork and slice about ⅛-inch thick circles. Taste a couple of slices to be sure the cucumber is not bitter. Cucumber sizes vary widely and I am broadly approximating 18 slices per cuke. If there are some really small ones, I like to overlap 3 slices per sandwich. Soak the cucumber slices in the vinegar and sugar while preparing the bread. Cut out the bread with a biscuit cutter. White bread will make a more delicate sandwich, but a nutty whole wheat can be quite nice also.

Spread the bread with the . Top with a slice of cucumber (blotted dry), salt, pepper, and dill. Cover with a slightly moist towel or napkin until ready to serve.

OPEN–FACE TOMATO SANDWICHES

{ MAKES 5 SANDWICHES. }

1 perfect tomato, never out of season
5 slices good white bread, preferably homemade
¼ cup Mayonnaise (see page 29, or Hellman's if it must be store bought; don't even
      think about reduced calorie mayo or I'll send the ghost of Grandmother out to
      haunt you!)
   Salt to taste
   Paprika to taste
   Black pepper to taste
   Cayenne pepper sparingly, if you like
   A sprinkle of fresh herbs (usually parsley or watercress, though basil has become the
      modern-day choice)

*C*ore the tomato and slash an X in the other end. Bring a pot of water to a simmer and drop the tomato in for about 20 seconds, until the peel starts to pull away. Be careful not to leave the tomato in for too long. It will quickly start to cook and get mushy. Use a slotted spoon to scoop the tomato out of the pot and place in a bowl of ice water. The peel should come off easily now. Slice the tomato into 5 slices and set aside.

    Use a biscuit cutter to cut the bread in circles the size of the tomato. Don't let the bread dry out at this point. Spread each circle with the mayonnaise, enough to be able to taste, but not so much as to squish out the sides of your mouth as you bite off a bit. Top with a tomato slice. Sprinkle with the salt and paprika, peppers, and the fresh herbs. These should, and will, be eaten within a couple of hours of preparation. Please avoid refrigeration. Cold temperatures turn a tomato's sugar into starch, hopelessly depriving the flavor factor.

MAYONNAISE

{ M A K E S   A B O U T   1 ½   P I N T S . }

3	egg yolks
1	teaspoon salt
1	teapoon dijon mustard
1	teaspoon chopped fresh garlic
½	teaspoon white pepper
¼	teaspoon paprika
	Pinch cayenne pepper
	Juice of 2 lemons
1	tablespoon roughly chopped flat leaf parsley
1½	cups vegetable oil oil

*P*lace everything but the oil in the bowl of a food processor fitted with the steel blade. Start the motor running and slowly pour in the oil. The mixture will emusify and thicken. Taste and adjust the seasoning.

WATERCRESS SANDWICHES

Peppery watercress grows wild in the streams of Middle Tennesse. Just don't mind the creek snakes and don't pick more cress than you intend to eat in a day or so. It will go limp and puny overnight.

{ MAKES ENOUGH FOR ABOUT 2 DOZEN SANDWICHES. }

½ pound fresh goat cheese (or cream cheese)
1 teaspoon grated onion
    Large bunch watercress (about ¼ pound, cleaned, stemmed, and coarsely chopped)
    Zest and juice from ½ lemon
    Freshly milled black pepper
    White or whole wheat bread

Mix together the goat or cream cheese, onion, watercress, lemon, and pepper. Let stand for 1 hour or so for the flavors to marry.

Spread the mixture thinly on the bread, which you may cut out however you choose. These sandwiches will keep well for a few hours.

COUNTRY HAM SANDWICHES

My great great grandmother, Kate Litton Cooper, recorded her version of this sandwich in her notebook, written in 1864.

{ MAKES ENOUGH FOR ABOUT 16 TEA-SIZED SANDWICHES. }

¼ cup Dijon mustard
½ cup butter, softened
1 teaspoon black pepper
    Pinch sugar
1 tablespoon cider vinegar
8 slices white bread
½ pound country ham, very thinly sliced
1 spring onion, sliced thin

Mix together the mustard, butter, pepper, sugar, and vinegar. Spread onto the bread and lay the ham on half the slices. Top with the onion and the remaining dressed bread slices. Cut into thirds.

SAUSAGE PINWHEELS

{ MAKES ABOUT 2½ DOZEN. }

1   recipe biscuit dough
½   pound breakfast sausage

$\mathcal{P}$reheat the oven to 400°. Roll or pat out the dough in a rectangle ¼-inch thick. Thinly spread sausage over all. Roll up jelly roll style to a log no more than 2-inches in diameter. Slice into ½-inch pieces. This is much easier to do if you first chill the log. Place on a lightly greased cookie sheet and bake for 15 minutes, until the sausage is cooked and the dough is lightly browned. Serve warm.

GINGER DATE NUT BREAD WITH CREAM CHEESE

This is a dense, nutty bread, not too sweet, that we spread with a mixture of cream cheese and butter. It may sound simplistic, but it is simply heaven. I'll bet that these are a British tea–time import. My fondest memory of this sandwich is as a munchy that my sisters and I nibbled on in the back of our big old Buick on the eight–hour drive to Florida. We never stopped for our big picnic lunch until shortly after we spotted the first Spanish moss in the trees. Just south of Op, Alabama, land of opportunity, to be exact.

$\mathcal{U}$se the bread recipe found on page 229. Slice thin and then cut in circles. Spread generously with a mixture of equal amounts of cream cheese and butter, and top with another bread slice.

OLIVES, DATES, OR ALMONDS IN CHEESE PASTRY

These used to be really popular, and I haven't seen them at a party in ages.
They're delicious, too, and very pretty.

$\mathcal{P}$reheat the oven to 350°. Use the recipe for cheese dough from the Marmalade Cheese Pastries (recipe precedes) and roll ¼-inch thick. Cut out pieces large enough to encircle your chosen filling and wrap them completely in the dough. Place on a non stick baking sheet and bake for about 15 minutes, until golden brown.

CHEESE STRAWS

I can't imagine life without cheese straws. Whenever I was living out of town and came home to visit,
Mama knew that cheese straws were the one food item that she must have waiting. I would walk in the house,
put down my bags, and proceed to the waiting tin on the kitchen counter. Having shoved several cheese straws
into my mouth, I was then prepared to greet the patiently waiting members of my family. First things first.

There are several variations of this recipe, some with sesame or benne seeds or even Rice Krispies
for crunch. My mother has always rolled the dough into a log, chilled the log, and then sliced off wafers
to bake. You can keep an unbaked log in the fridge for unexpected guests for at least a week or so. I have to admit
that I've always preferred the visual of the true "straw" that is run through a cookie press or else hand sliced in
strips and then cut into bite–size pieces. Whatever, I just crave the taste.

{ MAKES ABOUT 2 DOZEN. }

1½   cups all-purpose flour
1   teaspoon baking powder
½   teaspoon salt
¼   teaspoon or more cayenne pepper
½   pound sharp Cheddar cheese, grated
¼   cup butter, softened

Preheat the oven to 350°. Mix together first 4 ingredients and stir in the cheese. Add the butter and mix well. Finish in one of three ways:

1. Roll the dough into a log, 1½ inches in diameter. Chill, and then slice off ⅓-inch thick wafers.
2. Or run the dough through the #1 disc of a cookie press into long strips, directly onto the ungreased cookie sheet.
3. Or roll out in a rectangle about ¼-inch thick. Use a knife to cut strips the length of the dough, then slice these strips into about 2-inch pieces.

Bake for 15 to 20 minutes. The thicker straws will take longer.
Slice the pressed straws into 2-inch pieces while they are still warm.
Delicious warm or at room temperature. Stored in an airtight tin, these will keep for a few days.

MARMALADE CHEESE PASTRIES

The cheese and marmalade are so good together. This dough cooks more like a cracker
than the earlier cheese straws.

{ MAKES ABOUT 24 SMALL BISCUITS. }

1   cup all-purpose flour
½   cup butter, softened
¼   pound sharp Cheddar cheese, grated
2   tablespoons milk
¼   cup marmalade or jelly

Preheat the oven to 350°. Work together the flour, butter, and cheese. Mix in the milk to form a soft dough. Roll very thin on a floured surface and cut in small circles with the top of a spice jar. Use your finger to make an indentation and fill this with about ¼ teaspoon of the marmalade. Place on a nonstick baking sheet and bake for about 15 minutes, until the bottoms are browned and the marmalade is bubbly.

PIMIENTO CHEESE

I had always taken pimiento cheese for granted until I prepared some for a cross–cultural group of friends
residing in the Virgin Islands. No one from anywhere in the world except the South had ever heard of
pimiento cheese, and they all proclaimed me a genius for having created such a perfect food. Pimiento cheese
is a very handy trick if you should find yourself in a spot with limited groceries.

The most traditional way to eat this is stuffed in the hollow of a celery stick. The contrast in textures and flavors
is refreshing. It's also a nice filling for small tea sandwiches.

{ MAKES ABOUT 5 CUPS. }

1   pound sharp Cheddar cheese, grated
¼   onion, diced
¼   cup Mayonnaise (see page 29)
¼   cup buttermilk
1   2-ounce can pimientos, diced, the juice reserved
¼   teaspoon cayenne pepper

Combine all in a bowl and mix well. Pimiento cheese will keep in the refrigerator for several days. Allow to come to room temperature before trying to spread.

FLOWER SANDWICHES

When I really started exploring with cooking in the early eighties, I believed that edible flowers were just the epitome of moderne and sophisticated.

I have since found that every Southern cooking treatise I have read, from fifty to one hundred years old, uses nasturtiums, Johnny jump-ups, and borage in some very interesting ways. This idea is from my Aunt Kate Brew Vaughn. The peppery flowers are tasty with a mild cream or goat cheese.

{ MAKES ABOUT 36 SANDWICHES. }

  2 cups nasturtium flowers with several leaves
     Zest from 1 lemon
     Dash fresh squeezed lemon juice
 18 thin slices whole wheat bread
  1 cup fresh mild goat cheese (or cream cheese), softened

Roughly chop the nasturtiums with the leaves and toss with the lemon juice and zest. Cut the bread in small shapes, circles or rectangles, getting 2 small sandwiches from each larger slice of bread. Spread the bread with the cheese and and top liberally with the nasturtium mix, lightly pressing it into the cheese. Cover loosely with a towel until ready to serve. Serve within 2 hours of assembling.

ROLLED ASPARAGUS SANDWICHES

This is a classic Nashville appetizer from my childhood. I've updated a bit, using fresh asparagus (as opposed to canned), and homemade mayo instead of Miracle Whip. Pepperidge Farms makes the only bread I know of sliced thinly enough for these.

{ MAKES 24 APPETIZERS. }

12   slices Pepperidge Farm "Very Thin" white bread, (crusts removed, cut diagonally)
2   tablespoons Mayonnaise (see page 20)
24   pieces blanched asparagus
3   tablespoons melted butter

Preheat the oven to 400°.
  Spread the bread with homemade mayonnaise. Roll up the blanched asparagus in the bread. Brush with melted butter. Toast in the oven until the bread is firm and slightly browned.
  Serve at once.

SUN-DRIED TOMATO WHITE BEAN HUMMUS

Hummus is a classic Middle Eastern spread made with chick peas and sesame. Our white bean variation is more Mid–South in style, but still with a distinct Mediterranean flair. Great with pita chips, crudite, or spread on a chicken sandwich instead of mayo.

{ MAKES ABOUT 1 PINT. }

6   ounces sun-dried tomatoes, packed in oil
1   15-ounce can great northern beans, drained and rinsed
     Juice of 1 lemon
4   cloves garlic
1   teaspoon salt

Place all of the ingredients in a food processor, including the oil from the tomatoes. Process until smooth, adding additional olive oil if necessary.

YOGURT CHEESE

Evidence of a little Greek influence I picked up in culinary school, Yogurt Cheese is delicious, low fat, easy to make, and cheap! Add diced cucumber, garlic, and dill for an authentic Homeric delight. A little bowl of yogurt cheese, some yummy olives, a bowl of hummus, and some crackers or crusty bread make a simple, but sophisticated-looking appetizer for a summer afternoon.

{ MAKES ABOUT 1½ CUPS. }

2   cups plain, nonfat yogurt

Set a colander over a medium bowl. Line the colander with 2 layers of cheesecloth. Place the yogurt in the cheesecloth. Cover and refrigerate overnight. Discard the drained liquid.

BLUE CHEESE BUTTERMILK DIP

This little dip goes to almost every party I cater. Served with blanched asparagus or green beans, even carnivores eat their veggies!

{ MAKES ABOUT 4½ CUPS. }

2   cups plus 1 cup crumbled blue cheese
1   cup Mayonnaise (see page 29, or Hellman's)
1   cup sour cream
½   cup buttermilk
2   teaspoons fresh minced garlic
½   teaspoon cayenne

Place 2 cups of blue cheese and the remaining ingredients in a blender and mix well. Add additional blue cheese crumbles.

CORN CAKES

These hold up well enough to make a perfect hors d'oeuvre. I like to adorn them with a bit of barbecued pork and Chipotle BBQ Sauce (see page 181) or Peach Ginger Chutney (see page 25) with sour cream. A yummy little bite to act as a "base" for whatever you fancy.

{ MAKES ABOUT 6 DOZEN }

1 cup all-purpose flour
1 cup cornmeal
1 teaspoon baking powder
½ teaspoon baking soda
1½ teaspoons salt
¼ teaspoon black pepper
2 eggs, beaten
½ cup melted butter
2⅓ cup buttermilk
4 scallions, sliced thinly
    Kernels from 2 ears fresh corn

In a large bowl stir together the flour, cornmeal, baking powder, soda, salt and pepper. In a separate bowl mix together the eggs, butter, and buttermilk. Make a well in the dry ingredients, and stir in the wet, just to incorporate—don't overmix. Stir in the scallions and corn.

Heat a griddle or non-stick pan to medium. Add a little oil—just to coat—and spoon on batter by the tablespoon. When it bubbles up on the surface, flip and cook other side until light brown on both sides, about 1 minute on each. Serve immediately or let cool and re-heat on a prepared baking sheet in a 350° oven for 10 minutes.

BOILED PEANUTS

I've been told that boiled peanuts are an acquired taste, but I acquired it quite easily! They're common in South Carolina, and northern Florida where peanuts grow. Vacationers who frequent the Atlantic coast from Charleston to Jacksonville have doubtless seen them for sale in road-side stalls, right next to the peaches!

Their salty nature makes them a natural for snacking during the cocktail hour, and they also make a tasty addition to succotash. I've recently seen boiled peanuts popping up on menus at trendy beach-side restaurants, but they've been popular with the locals for ages.

{ MAKES 5 POUNDS. }

5   pounds raw peanuts in the shell
1   cup kosher salt

Rinse the peanuts in a colander. Place in a large stock pot along with the salt and cover with water. Bring to a boil and simmer until the peanuts are tender, about 30 minutes.

SPICED NUTS

What I love about this method is the lightness of the coating. There's no added fat to detract from the flavors of the nuts and spices, or to make your fingers icky greasy!

Play around with different spice combinations and different nuts.
We use these in salads, cheesecake crusts and pie crusts, and of course as a yummy snack on their own.

{ MAKES 1 POUND. }

1   pound whole nuts (almonds, pecans, cashews, walnuts, peanuts, or a combination)
2   egg whites
½   teaspoon salt
½   teaspoon cinnamon
½   teaspoon cumin
⅛   teaspoon cayenne pepper

Preheat the oven to 325°. Dump the nuts in a large mixing bowl. Add the egg whites and spices. Use your hands or long handled spoons to toss and coat thoroughly. Spread on a non-stick baking sheet and roast for 10 minutes.

BACON-WRAPPED CHEDDAR APPLES

For a little bitty hors d'oeuvre, they pack a lot of flavor into just a couple of bites—sweet and smokey, spicy, too. They are potentially messy bites, but decidedly worth the risk. Sometimes I leave off the cheese for a really fancy cocktail party, but I prefer parties where I'm comfy licking my fingers when I have to.

{ MAKES 24 HORS D'OEUVRES. }

 4   Granny Smiths (or other tart apples), cored and cut into equal wedges
12   slices smoked bacon, cut in half
½   cup light brown sugar
 1   tablespoon cracked black pepper
 1   cup grated sharp white Cheddar cheese

Preheat the oven to 400°. Wrap the apple wedges in half slices of bacon, tucking the edges under. Mix the brown sugar and pepper together in a small bowl. Dredge the wrapped slices in the mixture and place on a wire rack inside a baking sheet (with sides so the bacon grease doesn't run off!). Bake for 8 to 10 minutes, until the bacon is crispy. Remove from the oven and let cool slightly. Sprinkle each wedge with grated Cheddar before serving warm.

BLACK-EYED PEA SALSA

We have found this to be the perfect accompaniment to crawfish cakes, fried eggs, and a thousand other delights. The black-eyed peas give it a "down home" feel, but the flavors have a distinctly Latino beat.

You can use frozen black-eyed peas to make this throughout the winter months.

If you use canned roasted peppers, be sure they're really good quality. The freshly charred flavor derived from roasting your own peppers may make you decide to take the time and forgo the ease of the can.

{ SERVES 6 TO 8. }

1 pound shelled black-eyed peas
  Salt
2 bay leaves
1 tomato, diced
2 red bell peppers, roasted, peeled, seeded, and diced (see below, or 1 small can roasted peppers)
½ red onion, diced
4 cloves garlic, minced
3 tablspoons roughly chopped cilantro leaves

*I*n a large bowl combine everything and toss to mix well.

To Roast Bell Peppers:

On a grill: Cut away the stems, leaving the peppers whole. Wash the peppers, discarding any seeds. Pat dry. Prepare a hot charcoal fire. Place the peppers on an oiled grill over hot coals, turning often to lightly char the outside uniformly.

On a gas range: Turn a stovetop burner to high and char the pepper directly on the burner grate, turning often with long tongs.

In the oven: Cut the bell peppers in half lengthwise. Cut away and discard the seeds and membranes. Place the pepper halves skin-side up on a foil-lined baking sheet; flatten by hand. Broil 3 inches from the heat for 10 to 12 minutes or until blackened.

Place the roasted peppers in a resealable plastic bag, seal, and let stand for 15 minutes. (This will loosen the skins and make peeling them much easier.)

Peel and discard the skins. Store roasted peppers in an airtight container in the refrigerator.

GUACAMOLE

The last twenty years has seen this Mexican classic become a southern staple, too—so good with summer delights like corn and fresh tomatoes.

The cost of avocados makes this delicious salad/dip/topping a real luxury, but one I truly cherish. No matter how much I make, I never seem to have leftovers.

{ SERVES 6 TO 8 AS AN APPETIZER DIP WITH CHIPS. }

4	Haas avocados
½	ripe tomato, chopped
3	cloves garlic, minced
¼	red onion, diced
2	jalapeño peppers, seeded and diced
2	tablespoons chopped fresh cilantro
	Juice of 1 lime
¼	teaspoon salt

To dice the avocados, run a sharp knife through the skin and flesh, down to and all around the pit, cutting the avocado in half. With one hand on each half, twist and separate the halves. Carefully remove the pit and discard. Use a spoon to scoop out all of the flesh from the skin halves in one piece each. Now dice!

Toss the avocado into a mixing bowl along with the remaining ingredients. Stir and slightly mash with a spoon. If you are not using this immediately, you can squeeze a little additional lime juice on top, and place plastic wrap directly onto the surface to keep from discoloring. Refrigerate until ready to serve.

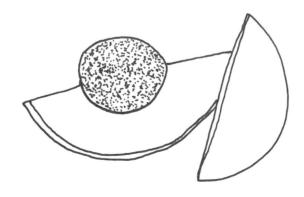

SMOKED TROUT SPREAD

This is a great spread to have on hand or mix up quickly. Simply put in a bowl and serve with crackers.

{ MAKES ABOUT 2 CUPS. }

8 ounces smoked trout fillet (pieces are o.k.)
2 ounces sour cream
1 ounce Dijon mustard
 Juice of ½ lemon
1 teaspoon fresh dill

In a medium bowl combine all of the ingredients. Mix well, breaking up the trout into flakes or small pieces. Refrigerate until needed. Keeps for several days.

CHEDDAR OLIVE SPREAD

I couldn't publish another book without this recipe. It's about as gourmet as I am (not).
May not be fancy, but you can stuff it in anything: celery, sandwiches, cherry tomatoes, perhaps;
and melt it over anything: grilled chicken or croustades or baked potatoes. You can even place it in a bowl
and heat it in the microwave. Give it a good stir (there's just a little bit of fat that might separate),
set it down with some chips, and voila! You're ready to entertain the world.

{ MAKES ABOUT 2½ CUPS. }

8 ounces (2 cups) grated sharp white Cheddar cheese
2 tablespoons Mayonnaise (see page 29)
½ cup chopped green pimento-stuffed olives
1 tablespoon brine from olives

In a medium bowl combine all of the ingredients. Mix well. Refrigerate until needed.

Beaten Biscuits and Country Ham

I feel compelled to take a deep breath before I utter the words "Beaten Biscuits." As if I were ambassador to some obscure country of which someone has politely made query. I'd better make what I have to say brief yet interesting and informative. Most unfortunately, in my own sentiments, at least, most folks just aren't interested in hearing as much about beaten biscuits as I know. It was a hard blow, coming to the realization of the greater public's apathy concerning beaten biscuits. You see, they are sacred in my family; to my mind, a good deal holier than that wafer that dissolved in my mouth at church on the first Sunday of every month. The breaking of beaten biscuits occurred with much greater regularity. My family is Methodist when it comes to communion wafers and grape juice, but quite Catholic in regards to beaten biscuits and iced tea. Growing up, we knew that not everyone had a beaten biscuit resource, and we pitied those unfortunates. After all, making Beaten Biscuits was not only an all day affair, but it required special equipment and skilled training. My grandmother and my mother both owned hand driven beaten biscuit cranks. Similar to pasta machines, but much more cumbersome, these had to be bolted to the kitchen table and required two healthy participants, one to feed the stiff dough through the rollers, and the other to catch the dough on the other side and ease the dough on the remainder of its journey. This process was repeated again and again until the dough "blistered" in a gentle puffing pop, indicating that virtually all air had been forced out of the dough. Once formed, the biscuits themselves were cooked in a very slow oven and allowed to sit in that oven until the oven was completely cool. "Light and airy" are not the adjectives one would choose to describe a beaten biscuit. No more so than "quick and easy."

Beaten biscuits originated when leavening agents were not available. Their utterly dry and dense texture was developed into an attribute rather than a liability, as workers would take the biscuits with them in their pockets as they rode through and labored in the fields. Beaten biscuits do not get stale. Back at the house, beaten biscuits were daintily served on silver trays with their match made in culinary heaven, country ham. Long after the introduction of soda and yeast made a softer, more delicate pastry possible, beaten biscuits remained the party biscuit of choice.

The cultural impact of the beaten biscuit in Middle Tennessee is best illustrated in a story my grandmother, Anna Martha Cooper Frost, born in 1887, used to tell me about an overnight party she attended as a teenager. As a means of amusement there was a competition to see who could make the best beaten biscuits without the aid of a biscuit brake. I guess they didn't have board games or Twister to entertain themselves. The ingenious young woman who won—my grandmother!—used a baseball bat to beat the dough into submission.

I have heard vague theories that beaten biscuits may have originated in England. If that were so, I believe that their American realm would cover much more territory, given the prevailing British influence throughout all of the colonies. Since at least the beginning of this century, beaten biscuits seem to have been peculiarly exclusive to Middle Tennessee and Kentucky. Mother was slightly disappointed at the blank faces of even my Virginia college chums and their families upon the presentation of the noble biscuit on parents' day weekends. Even more disheartening was the thank you note received from some new summer camp friends from Texas who exclaimed of the tastiness of beaten biscuits with jelly. Oh, dear. Oh, no, not jelly. Beaten biscuits are to be eaten with butter, butter and country ham, or plain. Jelly simply doesn't do.

As long as my grandmother was in the beaten biscuit-making business, my mother stayed out of the spotlight. But as Grandmother, then in her late eighties, stepped aside for the next generation, mother shone in her role as the High Priestess of Beaten Biscuits.

Mother's beaten biscuits are requested at every affair of cultural or historical impact. Country fairs, annual club picnics, study groups, garden club and church picnics. And that's just in the summer. We have them at Thanksgiving, Christmas, New Year's Day, and Easter, as well as most family birthdays, graduations, Christenings, and funerals, and of course in honor of the homecomings of displaced relations who have unwittingly wandered away from the bosom of the Tennessee Valley. This keeps mother busy.

When Aunt Mary Linda died, mother inherited her motor powered beaten biscuit brake. This ingenious machine is your standard biscuit brake driven by the horsepower of a Singer sewing machine. In the 1920s many ladies had their brakes thusly converted. I know of only two in existence today.

Mother set up the moterized brake in the play room, and Daddy was her able assistant. I don't know that this necessarily helped their relationship, but after forty-five years, they do what they had to for each other. After all, Daddy had the best beaten biscuit connection going. I think he was rather proud of tending the brake now and then.

BEATEN BISCUITS

There are a couple of variables here. Lard was originally used before we had vegetable shortening.
Lard will give a richer, fuller flavor, but many people prefer the cleaner taste from shortening.
Shortening is unquestionably healthier, but there are beaten biscuit purists who insist that
only lard will make a true beaten biscuit. The second variable is the sugar.
Mother changes the amount according to her mood. I lean toward the lesser.

You may use a food processor instead of a biscuit brake. My mother pooh-poohs the notion,
but I think that you will be pleased with the results.

{ M A K E S   A B O U T   4   D O Z E N . }

4   cups all-purpose flour
1   teaspoon salt
2   tablespoons cornstarch
1   to 2 tablespoons sugar
$2/3$ cup shortening (or lard)
1   cup half and half

Sift the dry ingredients together, and work the fat in as you would for a pie crust until the mixture resembles cornmeal. Mix in the half and half, and gather into a workable dough. Let rest in the fridge for about 30 minutes.

Preheat the oven to 300°. Run the dough through a biscuit brake several times, folding in half after each run, until the dough blisters. You should hear a little pop. If the dough cracks, pebbles, or is otherwise difficult before it blisters, let it rest for several minutes before continuing. Alternately, beat the dough with a rolling pin or baseball bat, or mix it in a strong food processor and let the dough run for a couple of minutes. This never fully works for me. I have to gather the dough from the bowl of the processor and work it together with my hands. The finished dough is very taut and smooth. Use a rolling pin to roll out about ½-inch thick. Cut in very small circles and prick each biscuit with the tines of a fork. Place on an ungreased baking sheet and bake for 30 minutes. Turn the oven down to 250° and bake for 30 more minutes. Turn the oven off and let the biscuits rest inside with the door closed until the oven is completely cold.

The biscuits split marvelously for spreading with sweet butter and filling with very thinly sliced country ham. As many times as I've had them, I salivate at the thought just like Pavlov's dog. Or is that Sarah's daughter?

STUFFED EGGS

No one in my family refers to deviled eggs, they are always simply stuffed. And a simple stuffing is usually the best. Mom used to try to sneak in a little curry powder, but Daddy would quickly call a halt to that nonsense.

{ MAKES 12 STUFFED EGG HALVES. }

6	eggs
1	tablespoon Mayonnaise (see page 29)
1	teaspoon Dijon mustard
1	teaspoon pickle relish
	Dash cayenne pepper
12	small sprigs dill
	Paprika

*P*lace the eggs in a pot and cover with water. Bring the water to a boil and cook for 10 minutes, boiling. Pour off the water and fill the pot with cold water. Let sit for 5 minutes. This makes the egg pull away from the shell, making them easier to peel.

Peel and rinse the eggs and cut in half lengthwise. Pop the cooked yolks into a mixing bowl and add the mayonnaise, mustard, relish, and pepper. Use a fork to mash the yolks, mixing them with the other ingredients. Taste for seasoning. Add a bit more mayonnaise if they seem too dry. If you make the mixture too wet, you can always cook some more eggs to add.

Use a teaspoon to refill the egg whites, mounding the filling up a bit. Garnish with a fresh dill sprig and a dash of paprika.

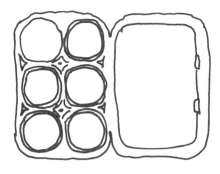

{ Chapter 3 }

SOUPS

One of my favorite chefs in culinary school has this to say about making soup, "If you think you are a chef because you can stick a piece of cow in the oven until it doesn't say moo, you got something to learn, my friend. Soup. That's where it shows if you know how to cook." While he is Italian and northern Italian at that, the art of soup making is a constant throughout the world. Soups have, should have at least, a subtlety that only happens through care, tasting, and a little intuition. Soups aren't as good if you just throw everything in the pot in no particular order and let her rip; and even when you follow a recipe ever so meticulously, you still have to stir and taste and make some decisions yourself. Whoever wrote that recipe you're using is probably not in your kitchen looking at those vegetables, tasting that chicken stock, stirring those beans. I believe that in good soup making a sense of devotion shines through, both to the soup and to whomever you're cooking it for. And I believe that kinder people make better soups.

Probably the most common Southern-style soup is a bean soup. Bean soups are practical. They're inexpensive, something you can make year round, and very filling—a point not to be overlooked if you have a big family or a few field hands to feed. No doubt these once all factored into the pervasive popularity of bean soups. But most of us today don't have to think too much about what foods are available at the market or what way to best fill several hungry tummies for as long as possible. These are, for the most part, affluent times, and bean soups the world around are essentially "peasant food." So there must be something more to this cheap and hearty fare, an essential ingredient not listed in many recipes, but definitely present in any pot of beans slow simmered in any kitchen. And that, my friends, is what I call soul satisfaction. That dreamy smile that wipes the frown lines away as you poke your head into the pot and lick your lips. The comforting sound your spoon makes scraping against the bottom of your bowl (especially when you know that there's more left in the pot). The warm glow inside your belly that spreads to all your toes and fingertips. That's the way a homemade bean soup should make you feel. And it feels even better to make one for someone you love.

I make bean soups with either fresh or dried beans. Obviously I use dried beans in the winter. I also tend to use dried beans for large batches of soup, as fresh beans are not so cheap as the dried variety. Frequently I use the traditionally Southern smoked pork seasoning when I make dried-bean soups. Smoked pork has been used as a seasoning in the South for centuries, lending a deep, distinctive flavor to so many dishes, particularly dried beans. The flavor of fresh beans themselves is so exquisite that I like to let the pure vegetable flavor shine through without any meat. Another variable in bean soup-making is whether or not to purée or strain the soup. I think that this is done more rarely these days, possibly being thought of as one more chore that could easily be cut out. While this is true, there's something so lovely about the velvety texture of smooth bean soup, and puréeing in a food processor will do the job almost as well as straining, and quite easily.

All that being said, I have included essentially three different methods for cooking bean soups. They may be varied by the other vegetables you use with the beans (bell peppers and carrots are two good options I didn't specify) and the type of beans you use. Beans all cook the same way, but they cook for different times, so beware. The idea of putting a pot of beans on the stove to cook all day without any attention is a myth. You must watch your beans and stir them now and then and occasionally add some liquid. Beans need attention just like everybody else. Enough already, here we go.

FRESH OCTOBER BEAN SOUP

A luscious soup that showcases the pure flavor of fresh beans. October beans are also known as cranberry beans.
They are fresh in season from late June to mid-September. The name "October?" Not quite sure.
Maybe that's when you dried them.

{ MAKES ABOUT 1 GALLON. }

2   quarts fresh October beans (or limas)
4   bay leaves
2   whole cloves plus 4 minced cloves garlic
3   teaspoons salt
1   gallon water
1   tablespoon olive oil
1   onion, chopped
¼   teaspoon black pepper
1   whole fresh cayenne pepper
2   fresh tomatoes, peeled and chopped
2   sprigs fresh thyme
4   sprigs parsley
½   bottle beer

Rinse the beans and pick over. Place in a pot along with 2 of the bay leaves, 2 whole cloves of garlic, and 1 teaspoon of salt. Cover with water. Bring to a boil and cook the beans until just tender, about 15 to 20 minutes. Drain and rinse briefly.

Heat the olive oil in a soup pot and cook the onions over high heat, browning them partially, for about 5 minutes. Add the minced garlic and cook for a minute, then stir in the beans. Cover the beans with about 3 quarts of cold water and add the other 2 teaspoons of salt, the black pepper, and cayenne. Bring to a boil. Reduce the heat, maintaining a slow but steady boil. Cook the beans for about 15 minutes, then add the tomatoes, thyme, and parsley. Cook for 30 minutes, then add the beer. Stir well and cook another 15 minutes.

If the soup is too thick, you may thin it with water or beer. If the soup is still too runny, let it cook down a bit more. Some of the beans should have fallen apart, thickening the soup, while a few whole beans remain. Taste the soup for seasoning and adjust. Remove the bay leaves, thyme sprigs, and the stems from the parsley. Serve the soup hot.

DRIED BLACK–EYED PEA SOUP

A great snowy weekend soup. Any leftovers help you make it through the following week.

{ Makes about 1 gallon. }

1   quart (2 pounds) black-eyed peas (white beans, kidneys, or pintos all work
      just as well)
1   pound pork trimmings (from country ham or hog jowl)
2   or 3 whole cayenne peppers, dried or fresh
2   bay leaves
3   quarts water
2   tablespoons olive oil
1   large onion, chopped
4   ribs celery, chopped
6   cloves garlic, minced
2   teaspoons dried thyme
2   teaspoons black pepper

Soak the beans in water overnight (this not only cuts down the cooking time, but also removes a lot of the material that causes gas).

The next morning, drain and rinse the beans. Place them in a large heavy pot along with the pork, cayenne peppers, and bay leaves, and cover with 3 quarts of cold water. Bring to a boil, stirring occasionally so that they don't scorch. Strain off the scum that rises to the top and turn down to simmer. Simmer until the beans are quite tender, and some have split open, thickening the soup.

While the beans are cooking, heat the oil in a skillet and sauté the onion, celery, and garlic with the thyme and pepper until the vegetables are translucent and slightly softened, about 10 minutes. Add these to the beans and cook about 30 minutes more. Remove the pork and skim the fat. Taste and adjust the seasoning, and serve with corn bread and hot sauce. Some people like to slice the pork thinly and serve the slivers on top of the soup bowl.

CREAMY WHITE BEAN SOUP

I like white beans to make a puréed soup because the skin of the bean is more tender to begin with
and white beans have a rich flavor that lends itself well to a smooth soup.

For a puréed bean soup, use the same quantities as for Black-eyed Pea Soup, simply substituting dried white beans for the dried black eyes. You might want to add 3 diced carrots to the vegetable mixture. They give the soup a little sweetness. Cook the vegetables in the olive oil, just as you do with the black eyes, then add the sautéed vegetables to the pot after 1 hour and cook them together with the white beans for 1 more hour. Remove the pork and either force the soup through a fine strainer or purée in a food processor or blender.
Return the soup to the pot and cook for another 20 minutes, stirring frequently. Adjust the seasoning and serve.

VICHYSSOISE

When I was a child, this chilled soup meant "ladies' lunch." Mama served dainty portions in pretty porcelain cups
with sterling spoons. It still speaks of white glove elegance to me.

{ MAKES ABOUT 3 QUARTS, 8 TO 10 SERVINGS }

1	pound red skinned or other waxy potato
	White part of 2 leeks, thoroughly rinsed and chopped
2	quarts good chicken stock
1	cup heavy cream
⅛	teaspoon ground nutmeg
	Snipped chives
	Salt and white pepper

Rinse the potatoes and place in a stock pot along with the chopped leeks and chicken stock. Bring to a boil, and cook until the potatoes are quite tender. Strain, reserving the chicken stock. Let the potatoes cool slightly and pull away the skin and discard.

Purée the cooked potatoes in a blender with the reserved chicken stock. Stir in the cream and nutmeg. Serve chilled garnished with chives.

COLD SQUASH AND BUTTERMILK SOUP

Consider this a summertime tonic. Refreshing, light, and zingy. A perfect lunch or early supper on the porch.

{ MAKES ABOUT 3 QUARTS. }

2	teaspoons vegetable oil
1	onion, diced
1	quart chicken stock, heated
1	teaspoon salt
½	teaspoon black pepper
	Pinch cayenne pepper
6	medium yellow squash (actually, the smaller the better—if quite small, use 8 or 10), scrubbed and sliced thin
2	cups buttermilk
1	tablespoon minced fresh dill
1	teaspoon minced fresh chives

Heat the oil in a saucepan and add the onion. Cook for 5 minutes, then pour the stock into the saucepan and heat to a boil. Add the squash and cook for 15 minutes. Remove from the heat and let cool. Roughly purée the soup in a blender or food processor, leaving some chunks. Pour into a bowl. Stir in the buttermilk and herbs. Let sit in the fridge for about 20 minutes, then taste and adjust seasoning. Serve cold.

COLD TOMATO SOUP WITH CUCUMBER AND MINT

It would be very pretty to use a variety of some of the different heirloom tomatoes that come in shades of yellow, gold, orange, and burgundy. A few farmers' markets or specialty stores supply them, or they're very rewarding to grow yourself. Each tomato variety has its own unique flavor and texture, as well as color, adding dimensions of interest to your summer as well as your soup.

{ MAKES ABOUT 2 QUARTS. }

4	ripe tomatoes, peeled, seeded, and diced
¼	red onion, diced
2	cloves garlic, minced
3	scallions, thinly sliced
1	cucumber, peeled, halved lengthwise, seeds removed, and thinly sliced
2	tablespoons fresh mint, roughly chopped
	Juice of 2 lemons
1	cup tomato juice
½	cup chicken stock (or water)
2	teaspoons salt
	Pinch cayenne pepper
½	cup sour cream or yogurt to garnish

Peel the tomatoes by first coring them, then dropping into simmering water for 30 seconds. Remove from the hot water and place immediately in ice water. Slip the skin off and squeeze out most of the seeds. Chop finely and place in a bowl with all of the juice from the tomatoes. Add everything but the sour cream. Stir and let sit for 15 minutes. Taste and adjust the seasoning. Serve chilled with a dollop of sour cream.

CABBAGE SOUP WITH ROOT VEGETABLES

This soup is so good and healthy. It's like a tonic to take the chill out your bones in the first promising days of spring.

{ MAKES ABOUT 1 GALLON. }

3	quarts chicken stock
1	medium potato, peeled and thinly sliced
1	medium turnip, peeled and thinly sliced
1	parsnip, peeled and thinly sliced
2	carrots, peeled and thinly sliced
2	teaspoons salt
½	teaspoon white pepper
2	whole cayenne peppers
3	bay leaves
2	tablespoons olive oil
3	strong spring onions (or 1 yellow), peeled, quartered, and thinly sliced
6	cloves garlic, minced
¼	green cabbage, sliced thin then chopped in bite-sized pieces
	Juice of 1 lemon
4	scallions, thinly sliced
1	sprig fresh parsley minced

Place the stock in a soup pot and bring to a boil. Add the potato, turnip, parsnip, and carrots along with the salt, pepper, cayenne, and bay leaves. Bring back to a hard boil and turn down to low.

Heat the olive oil in a large skillet and cook the onion over high heat for 5 minutes. Add the garlic and cabbage and cook on high, stirring, for 5 more minutes. Squeeze the juice from the lemon into the pan and remove from the heat. Place the contents of the skillet into the soup, stir, and let cook for 15 minutes. The root vegetables should be very tender and starting to break up. Retrieve the cayenne peppers from the soup, mince, and use as a garnish, if desired. Top with scallions and parsley. Sliced hard-boiled eggs and vinegar are also good ideas.

VEGETABLE BEEF SOUP

Browning the beef gives the flavor more depth.

That long list of vegetables is just the tip of the iceberg for what you could employ. In the winter you can use frozen vegetables, and in the summer you can clean out the garden, your fridge, and the fridge of all of your neighbors, if you choose. Think about trying eggplant, cauliflower, turnips and parsnips, beans, pasta, barley or rice, etc. There are no "correct" quantities, just what feels good to you, which may mean whatever you have on hand or something in the market that inspires you.
Be generous with the seasonings (and the love!). This will make or break your soup.

{ MAKES ABOUT 2 GALLONS. }

4   pounds beef for stew
1½ cups all-purpose flour, seasoned with 1 teaspoon salt and ½ teaspoon black pepper
5   tablespoons olive oil
1   cup red wine
1   gallon water
1   tablespoon salt
½   teaspoon black pepper
¼   teaspoon red pepper
2   bay leaves
2   onions, chopped
4   ribs celery, chopped
6   cloves garlic, minced
2   bell peppers, chopped
2   cups green beans, cut in 1-inch pieces
1½ cups corn kernels
1½ cups lima beans
2   medium potatoes, cut in 1-inch pieces
3   carrots, cut in 1-inch pieces
2   cups sliced okra
4   fresh tomatoes, peeled and chopped (or 1 large can)
2   cups chopped yellow squash
2   cups chopped zucchini
3   cups chopped cabbage
1   gallon beef stock
1   teaspoon oregano

1   teaspoon dried basil
2   tablespoons parsley
3   scallions, thinly sliced

*R*inse the beef and pat dry. Dredge in the seasoned flour. Heat 3 tablespoons of olive oil in a soup pot and brown the meat on all sides. If necessary, do this in batches to avoid overcrowding the pot. Pour in a little wine to help scrape up the browned bits on the bottom. Leave everything in the pot and cover with cold water. Add the salt, peppers, and bay leaves, and bring to a boil. Reduce the heat and simmer.

While the beef is cooking, heat the remaining butter in a skillet and sauté the onion, celery, and garlic for just about 10 minutes. Set aside. When the meat has cooked for 1 hour and 30 minutes, add the onion mixture along with the other ingredients, except the parsley and scallions. Bring everything to a boil and cook for another 30 minutes until the meat is very tender and the vegetables cooked through. Remove the bay leaf. The potatoes should start to break up a little and thicken the soup.

CHICKEN AND RICE SOUP

This is a wonderfully homey soup with terrific, rich flavor that can come only from making your own broth.

{ MAKES ABOUT 1 GALLON. }

1   whole chicken
2   ribs celery
1   onion, quartered
3   bay leaves
1   teaspoon dry thyme
1   tablespooon salt
1   dried cayenne pepper
½   teaspoon black pepper

1   onion, chopped small
2   ribs celery, chopped small
2   carrots, peeled and chopped small
1   red bell pepper, ribbed and seeded, cut small
2   teaspoons fresh rosemary leaves, minced

    Juice of 2 lemons
2   cups cooked rice
1   tablespoon fresh chopped parsley
4   scallions, sliced thin

Remove the giblets and discard or set aside for another use. Rinse the chicken well, inside and out. Place in a large pot with 2 ribs of celery, 1 onion, bay leaves, thyme, salt, cayenne, and black pepper. Cover with water. Bring to a boil, skim any scum that rises, stir, and reduce the heat to a simmer. Simmer the chicken uncovered for 40 minutes. Remove the chicken and let cool. Strain the broth, skim off as much fat as possible, and continue to simmer while you prepare the remaining ingredients.

Add the chopped onion, celery, carrots, bell pepper, and rosemary to the broth and cook for 40 minutes, until the vegetables are tender. Meanwhile, pull off the chicken meat and tear into slightly larger than bite-size pieces. When the vegetables are tender, add the chicken to the broth along with the lemon juice and the rice. Simmer for 5 minutes. Stir in the parsley and scallions and serve hot.

TOMATO BASIL SOUP

Probably the simplest (and most popular) soup to make. If you have time to "just heat something up,"
you have time to make this soup. If you really want to get fancy, you can add a drained can of
quartered artichoke hearts.

{ SERVES 4 TO 6. }

2	tablesoons olive oil
½	red onion, diced
5	cloves garlic, minced
2	28-ounce cans whole tomatoes, broken apart, with juice
12	ounces (1½ cups) tomato juice
1	cup heavy cream
¼	cup packed fresh basil leaves, torn in large pieces

Heat the olive oil in a large sauce pan. Add the onion and garlic and cook on medium heat for 5 minutes. Add the tomatoes with their liquid and the tomato juice, bring to a boil, and reduce the heat to low. Cook for 10 minutes. At this point, you can purée the soup to a smooth consistency, or leave it chunky.

Stir in the cream and re-heat (do not boil). Stir in the basil, season to taste with salt and pepper, and serve.

A little freshly grated Parmesan makes a nice garnish.

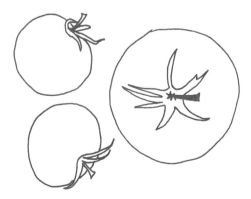

CREAMY WINTER SQUASH SOUP

This is soothing and creamy, but not too rich.

{ SERVES 8. }

3   acorn squash
6   tablespoons olive oil
    Salt and pepper
1   yellow onion, chopped
1   tablespoon chopped fresh garlic
1   tablespoon chopped fresh ginger
1   quart chicken or vegetable stock
1   can unsweetened coconut milk
2   tablespoons rice wine vinegar
    Chopped cilantro

𝒫reheat the oven to 375°.

Cut the squash in half. Scoop out the seeds. Drizzle about 3 tablespoons of olive oil over each cut side. Sprinkle with salt and pepper and place cut side down on a baking sheet. Bake until very soft, about 40 minutes. Remove and let cool.

Meanwhile, heat the remaining 3 tablespoons of olive oil in a large sauté pan. Add the onion and cook for 5 minutes. Add the garlic and ginger, and cook 5 minutes more. Add the stock and bring to a boil. Remove from the heat and let cool.

Working in 3 batches, scoop the squash pulp from the shells into a blender. Add ½ of the stock with vegetables and purée. Repeat with the remaining squash and stock. Pour the purée into a soup pot and heat. Add the coconut milk and rice wine vinegar, and heat through. Taste and adjust the seasonings. Garnish with cilantro.

SUCCOTASH

Succotash was originally a native American vegetable stew made largely of corn. Today there are many variations.
Succotash can be a hearty and comforting winter time meal made convenient and delicious with frozen corn,
or it can be a celebration of summer itself when the corn is high, the limas are fresh,
and the tomatoes are ripe. This is my summertime version.

{ Makes About 1 gallon, at least 12 servings. }

¼ cup olive oil
1 large onion, chopped
4 cloves garlic, minced
1 green bell pepper, ribbed, seeded, and chopped
1 red or yellow bell pepper, ribbed, seeded, and chopped
2 cups limas, rinsed
3 large tomatoes, peeled and chopped
2 teaspoons salt
½ teaspoon black pepper
¼ teaspoon cayenne pepper
   Kernels from 6 ears corn
2 tablespoons chopped fresh basil
1 tablespoon chopped fresh parsley
3 scallions, sliced thin
1½ teaspoons red wine vinegar
   Juice of 1 lemon

Heat the olive oil in a heavy pot or kettle and sauté the onions on high heat, browning them a little, for about 5 minutes. Add the garlic and peppers and cook for 5 more minutes. Stir in the limas and add water to cover, along with ½ teaspoon of salt. Bring to a boil and cook until the limas are just tender, about 10 to 15 minutes. Add the tomatoes with all of their juice, and the rest of the salt and peppers. Cook for 10 minutes, then add the corn. Cook another 10 minutes, then add the basil, parsley, scallions, vinegar, and lemon juice. Taste and adjust the seasonings. Serve as a stew over rice.

DUCK GUMBO

When my friends' father passed away last fall, the family asked me to prepare some food for a celebration of his life. Dr. Crenshaw lived his life to the fullest, and raised his four children to do the same. They're all avid outdoors enthusiasts, adventurers, and dare I say thrill seekers. (Courtney, who's my age, coerced me into illegally climbing fire towers at UVA, and that's a small adventure I can write about! There are others, which shall remain unspoken.)

Dr. Bill hunted, as well, and being the good steward, he ALWAYS consumed his catch. (There was that giant fish we baked at Carro's house in Destin... Remember, Court?)

A big pot of gumbo seemed a fitting tribute to this man's rich life, so I visited the Crenshaw's basement freezer and cleaned her out. Duck, quail, dove, and goose from Dr. Crenshaw's last hunts all found their place in the simmering pot.

The service was in Percy Warner Park, the day was brisk. Our hearts and bellies were full. This is an adaptation of what I made that day.

{ MAKES ABOUT 1½ GALLONS, ENOUGH FOR A CROWD OF 30 OR SO. }

1   whole duck, cleaned
1   quart mixed trimmings from onion, carrot, and celery
3   bay leaves
4   sprigs fresh thyme (or 1 teaspoon dried)
1   tablespoon salt
2   teaspoons black pepper

1   large yellow onion, chopped
2   green bell peppers, cored, seeded, and choopped
4   stalks celery, chopped
5   cloves garlic, minced
1   tablespoon Italian seasoning
½   pound (2 sticks) butter
1   cup all-purpose flour
1   gallon stock (from the duck)
1   28-ounce can chopped tomatoes
1   pound crawfish tails
1   pound andouille sausage, cut in circles
3   tablespoons filé powder

½   pound chopped okra
     Scallions
     Parsley

*R*inse the duck well. Place in a stock pot with the trimmings from the carrot, onion, and celery. Cover with water. Add the bay leaves, thyme, salt and pepper. Bring to a boil. Skim off the scum. Reduce the heat to low and cook until the duck is very tender, 1½ to 2 hours, skimming and stirring occasionally. Drain and reserve the stock. Pull all of the duck meat from the carcass and set aside.

In a large pot combine the prepared onion, pepper, celery, garlic, and Italian seasoning. Stir well. Cover and set over very low heat while you make the roux.

In a large skillet melt the butter. Whisk in the flour and cook on medium heat whisking constantly, until the mixture turns the deep color of an old copper penny. Be careful: it will not only burn, it will stick to your skin like lava. Remove the top from the pot of vegetables and pour in the hot roux. This makes one of my favorite sounds in the world. Smells pretty good, too. Stir a couple of times, then incoporate your hot stock into your roux, whisking. If you don't have enough duck stock, you can add shrimp or chicken stock. Bring to a boil, add the tomato, crawfish, andouille, and reserved duck. Bring back to a boil, and add the okra and filé. Return to a boil, stir, and turn to low. Cook about 30 minutes. Add hot sauce, salt and pepper to taste. Stir in the scallions and parsley. Serve over steamed white rice.

RED BEANS AND RICE

Red beans and rice is a Cajun classic that has become a staple in my kitchen, too.

{ SERVES ABOUT 8. }

1   pound red kidney beans (or the smaller "red" bean)
1   yellow onion, chopped
2   poblano peppers, stems and seeds removed, chopped
4   stalks celery, chopped
1   teaspoon Italian seasoning
1   pound andouille or kielbasa sausage, sliced in ½-inch circles
2   28-ounce cans tomatoes, broken apart, with juice
1   tablespoon salt
1   teaspoon black pepper
    Hot sauce to taste

Rinse and sort the beans. Place in a large pot and cover with water by twice the volume of the beans. Cover and soak overnight in the refrigerator.

Drain and discard the soaking water. Rinse the beans, place in a large heavy pot, and cover by twice their volume with water. Bring to a boil, skim the scum, and reduce the heat to low. Add the chopped vegetables and Italian seasoning and cook until the beans are tender, about 1½ hours.

Add the sausage, tomato, salt, and pepper and cook 30 minutes more. The cooking liquid should be a creamy consistency.

Serve over rice garnished with parsley, green onions, and hot sauce

MUSHROOM AND WILD RICE SOUP

Hearty without being heavy.

{ SERVES ABOUT 8. }

3   tablespoons olive oil
1   yellow onion, chopped
4   cloves garlic, minced
3   stalks celery, sliced thin
3   carrots, peeled and chopped
2   teaspoons Italian seasoning

1   quart mushrooms, sliced thin
2   quarts chicken stock
1   cup white wine
½   cup cooked wild rice
     Salt and pepper to taste
3   scallions, sliced thinly

Heat the olive oil in a heavy stockpot. Add the onions, garlic, celery, carrot and Italian seasoning, stir and cook 5 minutes. Add the mushrooms and cook a few minutes more. Add the stock and wine, and bring to a boil, reduce heat to low and cook about 20 minutes. Stir in the rice and lemon juice and heat through. Season to taste with salt and pepper. Serve garnished with scallions.

BROCCOLI AND CAULIFLOWER SOUP WITH CHEDDAR

A delicious way to eat your vegetables. This is a good way to use broccoli and caulilflower that may have gone a little limp.

{ SERVES ABOUT 12. }

3   tablespoons olive oil
1   yellow onion, chopped
1   head broccoli, broken into florets, with the tender stem chopped
1   head cauliflower, broken into florets, with the tender stem chopped
4   cloves garlic
2   quarts chicken stock
1   teaspoon Italian seasoning
1   cup heavy cream
     Salt and white pepper to taste
     Dash nutmeg
1   cup grated sharp white Cheddar cheese
     Croutons (see page 87)

Heat the olive in a heavy stock pot. Add the onion and cook 5 minutes. Add the brocolli, cauliflower and garlic, stir, and cook 5 minutes. Add the stock and It, seasoning and bring to a boil. Cook about 20 minutes, until the vegetables are quite soft. Let cool. Purée in batches in a blender. Return to the pot, stir in the cream and seasonings, and heat through. Stir in the cheese and heat to melt the cheese. Serve with croutons for garnish.

POTATO SOUP WITH BLUE CHEESE AND BACON

{ Serves 6. }

2   tablespoons olive oil

1   yellow onion, chopped

4   cloves garlic, minced

1   pound Yukon Gold potatoes, peeled and cut in chunks

2   quarts chicken stock

1   cup cream

½   cup crumbled blue cheese

6   slices bacon, cooked crispy and crumbled

4   green onions, chopped

Heat the olive in a heavy stockpot. Add the onion and garlic and cook for 5 minutes. Add the potatoes, and cover with the stock. Bring to a boil. Stir, reduce the heat to low, and cook for about 30 minutes, until the potatoes are very soft and broken up. Add the cream and blue cheese, and heat through. Serve garnished with the bacon and green onions.

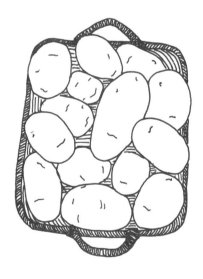

{Chapter 4}

SALADS

alads allow your creativity to fly. It's hard to tie a person down to a real recipe for a salad because so much depends on what kind of mustard happens to be in your refrigerator that day, what type of vinegar is open, how many bell peppers you have. These may account for subtle distinctions, but subtlety is what good food is all about. Changing a recipe doesn't necessarily make it worse or better; it does make it yours. All of these salads are things I have made countless times, probably never exactly the same way twice. I always encourage spontaneity, especially with salads!

PLANTATION SALAD

As in Belle Meade Plantation, where this salad is on the menu at Martha's. Tasty, hearty, low–carb… faboo!

{ MAKES 6 ENTRÉE SALADS. }

2   apples (I like Braeburn or Cameo), peel on, cut in 1-inch cubes
½   red onion, sliced thinly
1   tablespoon olive oil
½   teaspoon salt
¼   teaspoon black pepper
    Dash cinnamon

6   boneless, skinless chicken breast halves
8   ounces Brie, divided into 6 thinly sliced portion
9   ounces Burnt Sugar Vinaigrette (recipe follows)

*P*reheat the oven to 400°. Toss the apple and onion with the olive oil, salt, pepper, and cinnamon on a non-stick baking sheet. Bake for 10 minutes, until wilted and slightly browned. Set aside.

Season the chicken breasts and brush with a little olive oil (or use my marinade, page 180). Roast or grill for 10 to 15 minutes, until cooked through, but not dried out.

Remove from the oven and place the Brie on top of the chicken, allowing to slightly melt.

Toss the greens with the Burnt Sugar Vinaigrette, and divide onto 6 plates. Strew the apples and onions around the perimeter of each plate. Slice the chicken and place on top of the greens. Serve at once.

BURNT SUGAR VINAIGRETTE

{ MAKES ABOUT 1 QUART. }

1½   cups red wine vinegar
1   cup brown sugar
1   tablespoon fresh garlic
1   tablespoon salt
1   teaspoon black pepper
2   cups olive oil

*B*lend all of the ingredients together.

POTATO SALAD

I resoundingly believe that potato salad is best served while still a little warm. I love hot sauce on potato salad, or if I'm lucky enough to be at a barbecue, a bit of the barbecue sauce. I also know people who eat potato salad between slices of white bread, as a sandwich with catsup, and I know a couple of Cajuns who like to sink a spoonful of potato salad in their gumbo.

{ SERVES ABOUT 12. }

3   pounds potatoes, red or yellow thin-skinned variety, local if possible

½   yellow onion, finely diced

½   green bell pepper, diced

½   red bell pepper, diced

4   ribs celery, diced

4   scallions, cut thin

1   bunch parsley, minced

1   cup Mayonnaise (see page 29, or Hellman's)

½   cup mustard

1   teaspoon salt

½   teaspoon white pepper

½   teaspoon black pepper

¼   teaspoon cayenne pepper

¼   cup paprika

Scrub the potatoes, and cut into large pieces. Just cover with well salted water and bring to a boil. Boil about 10 to 15 minutes, until cooked through, but slightly firm to the fork. Drain, but do not rinse. Let cool. Combine the potatoes with the other ingredients in a large bowl. Stir to mix and adjust the seasoning.

The more you stir, the more your potatoes will mash. That's why I like to keep the potato pieces pretty large. They're just about salad size by the time you're finished mixing.

EGG SALAD

Makes a great sandwich with cucumber.

{ SERVES 4 TO 6. }

8   hard-boiled eggs, peeled and chopped
¼   red onion, diced
2   tablespoons Mayonnaise (see page 29)
2   tablespoons mustard
½   teaspoon fresh parsley or mint

*M*ix all together in a bowl. If the mixture is too runny, just boil some more eggs, chop them, and add to the salad.

COLE SLAW

Here in Tennessee, we like to put cole slaw on barbecued sandwiches. A must-have for a fish fry, too.

{ SERVES ABOUT 8. }

½   head red cabbage, very thinly sliced
½   head white cabbage, very thinly sliced
½   yellow onion, very thinly sliced
2   carrots, grated
3   scallions, thinly sliced
½   cup white vinegar
⅔   cup mayonnaise
⅓   cup Dijon mustard
    Juice of 1 lemon
¼   teaspoon white pepper
    Few squirts hot sauce
½   teaspoon salt

Mix everything together and adjust the seasoning and consistency to suit your taste.
    This recipe is kind of a mongrel. There are a million ways to make cole slaw. I took what I like best about several cole slaws and threw them all together.

TOMATO AND CUCUMBER SALAD

A classic summer salad. So refreshing.

{ SERVES 8. }

4	home-grown tomatoes, cored and cut into 8 wedges
2	cucumbers, peeled in strips and cut in ½-inch circles
½	red onion, very thinly sliced
	Juice of 1 lemon
2	tablespoons red wine vinegar
4	tablespoons olive oil
¼	cup mint leaves, cut in thin strips
½	teaspoon salt
	Several grinds black pepper

Toss it all together in a salad bowl and taste for seasoning. There's lots of room for experimenting with this recipe. Try lemon juice or a different kind of vinegar. Basil, dill, or cilantro instead of mint. I like feta cheese crumbled on top.

ASIAN CUCUMBER SALAD

This goes great with sesame noodles. Really refreshing with anything spicy.

{ SERVES 6. }

3	cucumbers, striped with peeler, sliced ¼-inch thick
1	vidalia or other mild onion, sliced thin
½	teaspoon salt
⅛	teaspoon red pepper flakes
2	tablespoons rice wine vinegar
1	teaspoon sesame oil
2	tablespoons chopped roasted peanuts
1	tablespoon chopped fresh mint

Toss all together in a mixing bowl and let sit about 30 minutes for the flavors to marry. Serve chilled.

TOMATO ASPIC

It took me years to find a tomato aspic I could proudly serve. This one is based on my grandmother's. It's very snappy and tasty, too.

{ SERVES 6 TO 8. }

1   package unflavored gelatin
¼   cup cold water
1   16-ounce can tomatoes
1   onion, sliced
3   ribs celery
1   teaspoon salt
1   tablespoon Worcestershire sauce
    Juice and zest of 3 lemons
¼   teaspoon cayenne pepper
¼   teaspoon black pepper
1   tablespoon chopped fresh basil
1   tablespoon chopped fresh parsley
2   teaspoons snipped chives

Soak the gelatin in cold water. Simmer together the rest of the ingredients except the fresh herbs until the tomatoes are thoroughly softened. Purée in a blender and pour over the gelatin. Stir in the fresh herbs and pour into a greased mold. Let set up in the refrigerator.

You may set pieces of cucumber and celery or whole peeled shrimp in the aspic. Push the garnish all the way to the bottom of the mold so that you can see it when it is unmolded. To unmold, wet a dishcloth with very hot water. Run this along the mold to loosen it. Place a platter over the mold and invert. If the aspic doesn't fall right out, continue rubbing a wet, hot towel over the mold until it loosens.

LIMA BEAN SALAD

This is a salad for July, for those few precious weeks when the fresh baby limas are out. When the good Lord provides a vegetable this sublime, you don't want to insult Him by messing with it too much.

{ SERVES 8 TO 10. }

3 pounds fresh baby limas, shelled and rinsed
   Water to cover
4 cloves garlic
2 teaspoons salt
1 teaspoon cayenne pepper
¼ cup best olive oil
   Juice and zest of 2 lemons
¼ cup fresh parsley, roughly chopped
½ bunch green onions, sliced thin

Place the limas in a pot and cover with cold water. Add the garlic, salt and cayenne and bring to a boil. Skim off the scum that rises to the top, stir, and turn the heat to medium. Cook uncovered until the limas are cooked through and tender, about 15 minutes.

Drain the limas, discarding the garlic cloves and bay leaf. Place the limas in a bowl and pour the olive oil over them while the beans are still warm.

Zest the lemons and squeeze the lemon juice into the bowl, avoiding any seeds. When the beans have cooled to room temperature, stir in the zest, fresh herbs, and cracked black pepper to taste. Check for salt and serve the beans at room temperature.

These can keep for several hours in the refrigerator, but be sure to bring them fully back to room temperature or the flavor will be greatly sacrificed.

BLACK–EYED PEA SALAD

This starchy salad can be a welcome change from the usual potato salad. Filling and fresh–tasting.

{ SERVES 12. }

3   pounds fresh black-eyed peas (or 1 pound dried)
1   gallon water
    Salt to taste
1   teaspoon white pepper
1   teaspoon black pepper
2   bay leaves
3   cloves garlic
    Juice of 2 lemons
2   tablespoons red winevinegar
2   teaspoons dried mustard
½   teaspoon salt
½   teaspoon black pepper
1   cup olive oil
1   sweet onion (Vidalia), diced
3   stalks celery, diced
2   home-grown tomatoes, chopped
½   cup chopped fresh basil
2   scallions, thinly sliced

If using dried beans, sort and rinse and soak overnight in water. Drain and rinse before proceeding. If using fresh beans, rinse and sort.

Bring water to boil with salt, peppers, bay leaves, and garlic cloves. Add the beans and return to a boil. Skim any scum that comes to the surface. Reduce the heat to medium and cook until the beans are cooked through but not mushy, about 1 hour and 30 minutes for the dried and 20 minutes for the fresh.

While the beans are cooking, mix together the lemon juice, vinegar, mustard, salt, black pepper, and olive oil as for a salad dressing.

When the beans are cooked, drain but do not rinse. Set in a large mixing bowl and pour the dressing over. Let sit until cool. Combine with the remaining ingredients and adjust the seasoning. The salad should sit for at least 30 minutes to allow the flavors to blend.

FRESH THREE BEAN SALAD

I have a strong hunch that before there were three cans of beans in the three bean salad, fresh October beans stood in the stead of pintos. Octobers are actually in season in July, right along with string and wax beans. This salad is an American classic which we need to rescue from the lame salad bars across the country. Let's get it out from behind that spit bar and back in the sunshine in the middle of the picnic table, proudly shouldering up to the potato salad and cole slaw.

{ S ERVES ABOUT 12 . }

1	pound fresh shelled October beans
3	cloves garlic, peeled
2	bay leaves
2	teaspoons salt
1	pound fresh snap beans
1	pound fresh wax beans
1	tablespoon salt
1	yellow onion, sliced in thin circles
3	stalks celery, thinly sliced on the bias
3	mild banana peppers, sliced in thin rings
½	cup olive oil
⅓	cup red wine vinegar
¼	cup sugar
	Black pepper to taste

Rinse the October beans and place in a pot. Cover by 4 inches with cold water and add the garlic cloves, bay leaves, and salt. Bring to a boil, skim the scum that rises, stir, and turn the heat down a bit. Continue to cook about 20 to 30 minutes until tender but not mushy. Drain and rinse under cold water, reserving the garlic cloves.

String the snap and wax beans. Bring a large pot of water with the tablespoon of salt to a rolling boil. Drop in the beans together and cook about four minutes, until crisp-tender. Drain and run under cold water until the beans are cool, to stop the cooking.

Place the three varieties of beans together in a large mixing bowl. Add the onion, celery, and peppers.

Mince the reserved garlic cloves and mix in a bowl with the olive oil. Pour the vinegar over the sugar and stir to dissolve. Whisk the vinegar and sugar into the olive oil. Pour the dressing over the vegetables. Taste, and add salt and black pepper to taste. Let the salad marinate for at 30 minutes before serving. Will last for 3 days in the refrigerator.

CORN AND GREEN BEAN SALAD

My favorite way to serve green beans on a late summer buffet. They're just too pretty for me to cook all day. Although I do love the way slow cooked beans taste, this is altogether different: vibrant with freshness straight from the field.

{ SERVES 6 TO 10. }

3   ears fresh corn, shucked and silks removed
1   pound fresh green beans, stem end removed
2   ripe tomatoes, diced
½   red onion, sliced thinly
1   cup Lemon Thyme Vinaigrette (recipe follows)

Bring 2 pots of salted water to a boil (one large enough for the corn). Add the corn and beans separately, and bring back to a boil. Drain the beans, and let the corn cook for no longer than 3 minutes, then drain. Run each under cold water to cool and stop the ccoking. Cut the kernels from the corn cob and place in a large mixing bowl with the remaining ingredients. Toss and let sit for 30 minutes to an hour to allow the flavors to marry.

LEMON THYME VINAIGRETTE

{ MAKES 1½ TO 2 CUPS. }

Juice of 6 lemons
1   cup olive oil
2   tablespoons honey
1   tablespoon fresh thyme leaves
1   teaspoon salt
½   teaspoon white pepper

Mix all the ingredients together well. I like to use a clean glass jar, screw the lid on tight and shake, shake, shake, shake!

SESAME NOODLES

Though decidedly exotic, sesame noodles are now standard fare in our take-out case and on many of our catering menus. The flavor is so bold and out-of-the-ordinary. Add a little something off the grill, and you have a really special meal.

{ SERVES 4. }

1	7-ounce package rice noodles
3	tablespoons soy sauce
3	tablespoons rice wine vinegar
2	tablespoons water
1	tablespoon sesame oil
2	tablespoons creamy peanut butter
1	tablespoon brown sugar
2	teaspoons grated fresh ginger
1	tablespoon minced fresh garlic
1	teaspoon crushed red pepper flakes
1/4	cup cilantro, chopped
6	scallions, thinly sliced
1	carrots, shredded
2	tablespoons black and white sesame seeds, toasted

Soak the noodles in boiling hot water for 5 minutes. Drain and rinse with cold water to cool. Set aside.

Combine the remaining ingredients in a medium bowl. Add the noodles, and toss gently to coat.

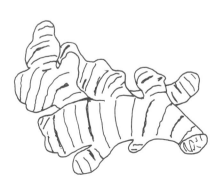

DIJON NEW POTATO SALAD

This is a French-style potato salad with a light vinaigrette dressing. Sophistacated enough to come to dinner with beef tenderloin, and equally at home on a barbecue picnic.

{ SERVES 6. }

2	quarts small red skin potatoes, cut in half
½	red onion, finely diced
3	stalks celery (hearts are fine), diced
2	tablespoons flat leaf parsley, coarsely chopped
1½	tablespoons Dijon mustard
1	tablespoon tarragon vinegar
¼	cup olive oil
1	teaspoon salt
½	teaspoon black pepper

Place the potatoes in a pot. Cover amply with water. Add about 2 teaspoons of salt and bring to a boil. Reduce to low and cook until tender, about 15 minutes. Drain (do not rinse).

When cool enough to handle, mix with the remaining ingredients in a large mixing bowl. Serve room temperature.

BEET AND NEW POTATO SALAD

Many of the "composed" salads from our Southern heritage are a bit long on the mayonnaise and sugar for most contemporary tastes—mine at least. That said, I was delighted to discover some suggestions from the last century for really exciting combinations for cold salads. One of my favorites is a lusty and satisfying marriage of beets, new potatoes, and hard-boiled eggs. This is a visual feast, as well.

{ SERVES 6 TO 8. }

1   pound fresh beets
1   pound new potatoes
2   small spring onions, cut in thin circles
6   eggs
1   large bunch watercress
1½ cups True French Dressing (recipe follows)

Trim the beets and boil in salted water about 15 minutes until tender. Cooking time will vary with their size and freshness. When they are easily pierced with a fork, drain and let cool. When they are cool enough to handle, peel (the skins slip off fairly easily) and slice in halves or quarters, depending on their size. Don't worry, the pink on your hands will eventually wash away.

Scrub the potatoes clean and cut in halves or quarters, depending on their size. Boil in salted water until tender but not mushy, about 10 to 15 minutes. Drain and set aside.

Place the eggs in a pot and cover with water. Bring to a boil and cook for ten minutes, boiling. Drain off the water, leaving the eggs in the pot. Refill with cold water. Set aside.

Pick through and rinse the watercress.

Place the potatoes, onions, and beets in a large mixing bowl and pour the dressing over. Toss the salad, watching the onions and potatoes turn intriguing shades of pink. Let the salad marinate in the dressing for at least 30 minutes.

Peel the eggs and cut lengthwise into quarters. Lay the watercress on a platter and mound the salad on top. Garnish with the egg wedges and grind some black pepper on top.

TRUE FRENCH DRESSING

Most Southerners, with the exception of the Cajuns and Creoles, have not traditionally used a lot of garlic.
Raw garlic, and in some cases raw onion, was considered, well, impolite. Recipes that did use garlic would
frequently call for merely rubbing the salad bowl with the crushed clove. That doesn't quite get it for me.
I say chop it up and toss it in. Life's just too short.

{ MAKES ABOUT 1½ CUPS. }

¼   cup vinegar (white or red wine)
    Juice of 1 lemon
1   tablespoon grated onion
1   clove garlic, well minced (optional)
1   teaspoon minced fresh parsley
1   teaspoon paprika
1   teaspoon dry mustard
1   teaspoon salt
1   cup olive oil

Mix the vinegar with the spices and beat in the olive oil. Let sit for 30 minutes before using.

PICKLED BEET SALAD

Keep some in the fridge to perk up any meal in a hurry.

{ SERVES 6 TO 8. }

2   pounds fresh beets
2   small white onions, very thinly sliced into circles
¾   cup white vinegar
    Pinch salt
    Pinch cayenne pepper

To cook fresh beets, which have much more flavor than canned ones, first rinse the beets well. Then trim both ends of the beets and boil in salted water for about 25 minutes, until fork tender. Drain and cool, then rub the skin away. Slice the beets in ½-inch circles. Toss with the remaining ingredients and let stand at least 1 hour to let the beets marinate.

MARINATED BRUSSELS SPROUTS

I know that I emote a lot about a lot of vegetables, but I really, really love Brussels sprouts. Imagine, little mini cabbages growing on a bush! To put a whole Brussels sprout in your mouth and bite through all of that pungent flavor and goodness. How did God come up with this stuff? This salad helps get me through the winter blues. I found one very similar in some family writings from the turn of the century.

{ SERVES 6. }

2   pounds fresh Brussels sprouts
3   quarts water
2   teaspoons salt
1   tablespoon capers, chopped
2   scallions, thinly sliced

2   cloves garlic, minced
3   tablespoons red wine vinegar
1   teaspoon dry mustard
½   teaspoon crushed black pepper
    Additional salt, as needed
    Juice and zest of 1 lemon
½   cup olive oil

Clean and trim the Brussels sprouts and cut in half, lengthwise. Bring the water to a boil with the salt and add the Brussels sprouts. Bring to a boil and cook until tender, about 5 minutes. Drain the sprouts and run under cold water. Place in a bowl with the capers and scallions.

In a separate bowl whisk together the remaining ingredients except the oil. Pour the oil into the rest, whisking until emulsified. Pour the dressing over the salad. Taste and adjust seasoning. Let the salad sit for at least 30 minutes to allow the flavors to marry. Serve at room temperature.

CRANBERRY SALAD

I like this better than traditional cranberry sauce for Thanksgiving and Christmas. It's more of a relish than a salad.
Delicious with my favorite deep fried turkey (I like the dark meat best.)

{ SERVES 4. }

2   cups washed raw cranberries
2   cored apples, cut in medium chunks
1   large seedless orange, cut into 8 sections
2   cups sugar

*U*se a food processor to grind up the mixture (yes, you leave the peel on the orange!), pulsing as needed. Remove to a boil and let the mixture sit for 30 minutes or more to let the flavors come together.

APPLE AND WALNUT SALAD WITH BLUE CHEESE DRESSING

This a beautiful autumn salad. Perfect for a luncheon or for a light supper.

{ SERVES 4. }

2   apples, fresh tart locals or Granny Smith
1   stalk celery, thinly sliced
    Juice of ½ lemon
½   bag spinach, cleaned and trimmed
½   cup black walnut pieces (English walnuts may be used; black walnuts are hard to
        find)
4   scallions, thinly sliced
½   cup Blue Cheese Dressing (recipe follows)

*R*inse the apples and slice in thin wedges, leaving the peel intact. Toss with the celery and lemon and set aside.

Preheat the oven to 400°. Place the nuts on a baking sheet and roast for about 5 minutes. Careful, they burn really easily.

Divide the spinach between 4 salad plates and casually arrange the apples on top. Sprinkle nuts and scallions over and drizzle with Blue Cheese Dressing.

BLUE CHEESE DRESSING

This old-fashioned blue cheese dressing has a devoted following. This is a classic for a reason: it's just so darned tasty.

{ MAKES A LITTLE OVER 1 CUP. }

- 6   tablespoons blue cheese
- ½   cup olive oil
- 1   clove garlic, minced
- ¼   teaspoon white pepper
- ¼   teaspoon paprika
- ½   teaspoon salt
- 3   tablespoons vinegar

Crumble the cheese and mix into the oil. Mix the garlic and seasonings into the vinegar. Pour the oil into the vinegar, stirring well.

POPPY SEED DRESSING FOR FRUIT SALAD

Fruit salad should be as seasonal as the farmers' market. Apples, pears, and citrus are natural in cold weather months, while melons and berries shine in the summer. This traditional dressing works in all seasons.

{ MAKES ABOUT 1 PINT, ENOUGH FOR 12 TO 16 SERVINGS OF FRUIT. }

- ½   cup sugar
- ⅓   cup red wine vinegar
- 1   teaspoon dry mustard
- 1   teaspoon salt
- 1   teaspoon paprika
- 1   cup vegetable oil
- 2   tablespoons poppy seeds

Mix the sugar with the vinegar to dissolve. Stir in the mustard, salt, and paprika. Whisk in the oil and stir in the seeds. Whisk together briskly before serving.

PINK POPPY SEED VINAIGRETTE

You can make the dressing without the beet "juice," but it won't be pink! Simply not the same,
to my way of thinking, and who wouldn't benefit from having some pickled beets on hand?
(I suppose you could always buy a can.)

I love this over fresh melon with a bit of briny feta cheese.

{ MAKES ABOUT 4 CUPS }

1½ cups red wine vinegar
½   cup sugar
2   teaspoons minced fresh garlic
2   teaspoons salt
2   teaspoons Dijon mustard
1   teaspoon white pepper
1   egg yolk
2   cups vegetable oil
4   tablespoons poppy seeds
1   tablespoon juice from "pickled beets"

Place everything but the oil, poppy seeds, and pickle juice in a blender. Start the blender and pour in the oil, blending to a creamy consistency. Add the poppy seeds and pickle juice to a tasteful blushing pink shade, and blend lightly.

CHICKEN SALAD

To this day, every day, I am newly astonished at just how much chicken salad people that live around here can and will eat. It boggles the mind. Needless to say, the "correct" chicken salad is a topic of heated dispute. For example, my mother uses a boiled dressing, which she will swear to you is the only honorable way to dress chicken salad. Sorry Mom, I like mine better, and it's much easier, too.

Although I am a thigh–eater at heart, I use only white meat for traditional Southern chicken salad. I like the milder flavor with the other simple ingredients.

This is a very basic chicken salad recipe. It can be gussied up for a fancier occasion with toasted sliced almonds or walnut halves and halved grapes. This version is nice in a lettuce cup with some finger sandwiches for a luncheon.

In our neck of the woods, you will find chicken salad between slices of bread, in a tomato, in an avocado half, in a hollowed out pineapple wedge and stuffed in pastry puffs, and almost always inside almost every refrigerator.

{ SERVES ABOUT 12 TO 16. }

8   chicken breasts, bone in and skin on (this will give more flavor, but in a big hurry, use boneless-skinless and cut down the cooking time)
½   teaspoon salt
¼   teaspoon white pepper
¼   teaspoon black pepper
     Pinch cayenne pepper
1   teaspoon fresh thyme leaves (or ½ teaspoon dried)
2   cloves fresh garlic, thinly sliced
3   stalks celery, finely chopped
¼   red onion, finely chopped
¼   cup Mayonnaise (see page 29)
⅓   cup buttermilk
1   tablespoon dijon mustard
1   tablespoon chopped fresh parsley

Rub the chicken breasts with the salt, peppers, and thyme, getting up under the skin, and push the garlic slices under the skin as well. Pull the skin back over the flesh and roast the breasts at 400° for 20 or so minutes, until cooked through and the juices run clear. Do not overcook.

When cool enough to handle, remove the skin and discard. Discard the garlic slices. Pull the meat from the bone, tearing into larger than bite-sized pieces, not too small. Mix with the remaining ingredients.

MARINATED SHRIMP SALAD

I love this salad in the heat of the summer. No matter how wilted people may feel, they can always eat shrimp.
They can eat quite a lot of shrimp, as a matter of fact. I always make more than I think I could
possibly need, and I never have leftovers.

{ SERVES ABOUT 6 AS A MAIN COURSE. }

3 pounds shrimp
1 gallon water
2 lemons, cut in half
2 green onions, roughly chopped
3 sprigs parsley
1 celery stalk, chopped
1 bay leaf
2 teaspoons black pepper
1 teaspoon cayenne pepper

½ cup good olive oil
1 tablespoon white wine vinegar
4 lemons, juiced and zested
3 cloves garlic
¼ to ½ teaspoon black pepper
1 ounce fresh parsley leaves
½ ounce fresh dill
  Salt to taste
½ red onion, finely chopped
3 stalks celery, diced
1 red bell pepper, diced
1 banana pepper (or hot pepper), seeded and finely chopped
1½ tablespoons capers, roughly chopped

*R*inse the shrimp. Bring the water to a rolling boil with 2 lemons, green onions, parsley sprigs, 1 celery stalk, bay leaf, and black and cayenne pepper. Throw in the shrimp and bring back to a boil. Cook for about 4 minutes. You can tell that the shrimp are done when the meat pulls slightly away from the shell. Don't overcook!

When the shrimp are cooked, pull the pot from the heat and throw ice into the water to stop the cooking. This way the shrimp are still soaking up the flavors of the liquid without overcooking. If the ice melts very quickly add some more. You can drain and peel the shrimp in about 5 minutes.

Place the olive oil, vinegar, lemon juice, lemon zest, garlic, black pepper, parsley, dill, and salt to taste in the blender and purée until combined and smooth. Cut the shrimp in a little larger than bite-size pieces and place in a glass or ceramic bowl along with the remaining salad ingredients. Pour the dressing over and toss. The amount of salt you will need for the dressing depends on the saltiness of the shrimp. Some shrimp will be very salty when you purchase it, others not. You'll have to taste for yourself.

This salad is so refreshing, it's perfect for summer, served with avocados or tomatoes, or simply on a bed of lettuce. The flavor will improve for several hours after marinating, but it should be eaten by the following day.

BEACH CLUB SHRIMP SALAD

A lovely treat when you're not at the beach, too! Nothing trendy here, just classic yumminess.
Note: it will be much yummier if you boil your own shrimp (see page 85) rather than buying the icky
pre-cook rubbery stuff from the store—not that I have an opinion or anything.

{ SERVES 4 TO 6. }

2 pounds boiled large shrimp, peeled and de-veined, tail-off
½ cup Mayonnaise (see page 29)
½ cup sour cream
1 tablespoon Dijon
1 tablespoon capers
3 stalks celery, minced
1 tablespoon chopped flat leaf parsley

Chop the shrimp into bite-sized pieces and place a bowl with the remaining ingredients. Mix well and adjust the seasoning.

TUNA SALAD

A lot of folks are really hooked on our tuna salad. It's light and lemony.
Perfect for lunch or a simple summer supper.

{ S E R V E S   4 . }

1	can albacore tuna (or pouch)
3	stalks celery, diced
1	tablespoon minced red onion (optional)
1	cup mayonnaise
1	tablespoon Dijon mustard
	Juice of 1 lemon
1	tablespoon capers
½	teaspoon dried dill
	Pinch cayenne

Drain the tuna well, place in a mixing bowl, and flake thoroughly. Add the remaining ingredients and mix well.

THE WEDGE

My take on a another seventies classic. While perhaps not as "interesting" as the now ubiquitous
"mixed maybe greens," the old iceberg wedge is miraculously refreshing. We douse it in garlic-y blue cheese dressing,
add bacon bits, hard boiled egg, and, of course, I like pickled beets.
Add a scoop of chicken, tuna, or egg salad if you need a protein boost.

{ S E R V E S   4 . }

1	head iceberg lettuce
	Buttermilk Blue Cheese Dressing (recipe follows)
6	slices bacon, cooked, cooled and crumbled
3	hard boiled eggs, chopped
2	cups Croutons (recipe follows)
1	cup pickled beets (optional)

Core the iceberg, cut into 4 wedges, and place each on a plate. Liberally top with dressing (the lettuce seems to drink it up) and garnish with the remaining ingredients. Serve immediately.

BUTTERMILK BLUE CHEESE DRESSING

{ MAKES ABOUT 1½ CUPS. }

½ cup crumbled blue cheese
¼ cup sour cream
¼ cup mayonnaise
¼ cup buttermilk
1 teaspoon chopped fresh garlic
    Pinch cayenne
    Salt to taste

Mix together in a blender or by hand with a whisk.

CROUTONS

1 inch bread cubes
    Olive oil
    Salt
    Black pepper
    Granulated garlic
    Italian seasoning

Preheat the oven to 350°.
  Toss the cubed bread on a baking sheet along with the other ingrecients, coating the bread evenly and thoroughly. Bake for 10 to 15 minutes, tossing once with a spatula midway through. Cool and store in an airtight container.

GREEK ORZO (PASTA) SALAD

{ Serves 6 to 8. }

  2 cups orzo (rice-shaped) pasta
  2 teaspoons salt
¼ cup olive oil
½ cup crumbled feta cheese
  2 to 3 stalks celery (hearts are fine), thinly sliced
¼ red onion, thinly sliced
     Juice and zest of 1 lemon
  1 teaspoon minced fresh garlic
  2 tablespoons chopped flat leaf parsley
¼ cup pitted kalamata olives, sliced in half
  2 scallions, thinly sliced
¼ cup jarred pepperoncini peppers, stems removed, thinly sliced
  1 tablespoon capers
  1 tablespoon tarragon or white vinegar
½ teaspoon salt
     Pinch red pepper flakes

Bring a pot of water to boil with 2 teaspoons of salt. Add the orzo and stir. Turn to medium and cook to al dente about 5 minutes. Drain and rinse to cool. Shake out the excess water and place the orzo in a mixing bowl with the remaining ingredients. Stir to mix. Season to taste. Best served that day or the next.

{ Chapter 5 }

VEGETABLES AND SIDES

A Southern table is made heavy by the vegetable dishes and side items. Traditionally, meat may be scarce, but greens, cornmeal, and potatoes rarely are. For centuries Southern cooks have used their ingenuity and imagination to concoct a startlingly vast and varied array of offerings made from what nature, a little farming, and some milling could provide. A hearty Southern dinner would have five or six side dishes, plus some sliced tomatoes and onions and a pickle tray. I have gone through the alphabet, filing my vegetables and sides accordingly. I could go back through and write about twice as many. But then what would I write about next time? These should provide a little inspiration. Starting with "A:"

SIMPLE ASPARAGUS

Asparagus is wildly popular with my friends, family, and clients. I don't believe that we have quite adapted to the year round availability of the vegetable and, unlike many grocery store staple vegetables, which are too often woody and bland, we still rightly value asparagus as a precious object. Even though I can find it in my grocery store any time, I most treasure the taste of asparagus in the spring, when the earth is fresh and green and the first sprouts and bittersweet vegetables are bursting into our lives. Everyone cooked their asparagus a good deal longer twenty, even ten years ago. But now, all the folks I encounter, with the exception of my father, prefer their asparagus lightly cooked.

{ SERVES 6 TO 8. }

2   bunches asparagus
1   gallon water
1   tablespoon salt
1   gallon ice water
2   teaspoons butter
1   teaspoon fresh dill

Snap the asparagus stalks off just above the woody ends and discard ends. Bring the water to boil with the salt. Drop the asparagus in and let cook for 1 or 2 minutes after the water has regained its boil. Strain off the asparagus and toss it with the butter and dill. Serve immediately.

If you are not serving right away, plunge the cooked asparagus into ice water after it is drained. To serve, strain from ice water and reheat in a pan with melted butter until warm through. Toss with dill and serve.

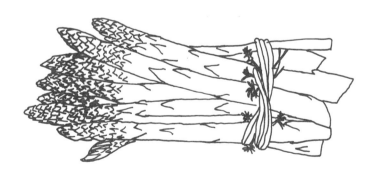

MARINATED ASPARAGUS

This is a marvelous picnic or party item. I strongly urge considering asparagus a finger food.
Its much more fun that way. The longer the asparagus sits in the marinade, the less vibrant its green color.
As a trade off, the yummy taste of the marinade becomes more pronounced.

{ SERVES 6 TO 8. }

1   gallon salted water
2   bunches asparagus
1   gallon ice water

½   cup olive oil
½   cup white wine vinegar
     Juice of 1 lemon
½   teaspoon salt
½   teaspoon cracked black
       pepper
1   clove garlic, minced
1   teaspoon chopped fresh dill
1   teaspoon chopped fresh mint
1   teaspoon chopped fresh
       parsley

Bring the salted water to a boil (salt not only flavors the asparagus, it enhances the bright green color). Add the asparagus and cook for just 1 to 2 minutes. Drain and plunge the asparagus into ice water to stop the cooking.

Mix together the remaining marinade ingredients and pour over the drained asparagus in a noncorrosive container. Allow the asparagus to sit in the marinade for at least 30 minutes and up to 2 hours, depending on how concentrated you care for the flavor to be. If you refrigerate, allow to come to room temperature before serving.

ASPARAGUS GRATIN

YES! Fresh farm cheese, cow and goat, was common in the South and most of the nation before the depression and the general move away from individual farms and towards large corporate dairies. Most farm wives made their own simple, mild cheese with the curds left over after milking.

In the last few years the face of cheese making has changed dramatically in this country. Once again there are small dairies scattered across the country, free-grazing their own herds of cattle, goats, or sheep, and producing everything from organic milk and butter to fresh, hand-ladled cheeses and more complex cooked and aged cheeses—a huge variety. In some communities local cheeses are found at the farmers' markets, while many gourmet grocers seek out these artisan cheeses. Seek out a few yourself. Smell and taste, and celebrate the notion of thinking small and taking a few steps backwards now and then!

{ SERVES 6. }

1	gallon salted water
2	bunches asparagus
1	tablespoon chervil or parsley
⅔	cup cream
½	cup fresh goat cheese, or grated cheese of your choice
1	tablespoon minced chives
	Salt and black pepper

Snap off the asparagus just above the woody ends. Bring the salted water to a boil and cook the asparagus for 2 minutes. Drain. Lay the asparagus in a casserole. Stir the chervil into the cream and pour the cream over the asparagus. Dot with goat cheese and sprinkle the chives over. Bake at 400° for 10 to 15 minutes, until the cream is thickened. If the cheese is not browned, turn your oven setting to broil and brown the top of the gratin for about 5 minutes. Serve at once.

Chervil is a delicate herb I like to use, especially in the spring. Mint, dill, or parsley would all be good substitutes if you can't find the chervil.

BAKED BEANS

While a smoking grill can make your patio smell like the Fourth of July, baked beans will do the same for your kitchen. These are a little sweet, a little tangy, rich and flavorful. Don't save them for just one day.

{ SERVES 12. }

1	28-ounce can pintos, drained
1	28-ounce can white kidneys, drained
6	slices bacon
1	yellow onion, diced
1	green bell pepper, diced
1	red bell pepper, diced
5	cloves garlic (or more), minced
3	tablespoons tomato paste
¼	cup yellow mustard
¼	cup molasses
¼	cup firmly packed dark brown sugar
1	tablespoon vinegar cayenne hot sauce (such as Crystal)
2	teaspoons cider vinegar
1	teaspoon Worcestershire sauce
½	teaspoon salt
½	teaspoon black pepper

Drain and rinse the beans well. Combine the beans in a large mixing bowl and set aside.

Cook the bacon in a skillet until crispy. Pull out the bacon and drop in the onions. Cook in the bacon drippings until translucent, then add the peppers and the garlic. Cook just to wilt the vegetables, 5 or so minutes. Add the vegetables to the beans, along with remaining ingredients except the bacon. Mix, taste, and adjust to suit you. Pour into a casserole, cover, and bake at 350° for 40 minutes.

Remove the cover and crumble the bacon on top. Put back in the oven, uncovered, for 10 more minutes.

COUNTRY–STYLE GREEN BEANS

{ S ERVES 8 . }

3   pounds fresh green or pole beans, stringed
⅓   pound country ham or fat back
1   yellow onion, sliced
2   pods dried cayenne pepper
1   tablespoon salt
6   new potatoes, quartered
    Vinegar

$\mathcal{P}$lace the beans, ham or fat back, and onion in a stock pot, along with the cayenne and salt. Cover with cold water and bring to a boil. Turn to low heat and cook until the beans are very tender, 1 hour or so. Add the potato quarters and cook until tender, another 20 minutes. If you like, remove the ham, cut or tear into small pieces, and put back in the pot.

The "pot licker" from this dish is so good, you may like to serve the beans in a bowl, along with corn bread to mop up that tasty juice.

GREEN BEANS WITH CHILI SAUCE

This was the "city" way to serve green beans in my home.

{ S ERVES 6.}

2   pounds green beans, stringed and cleaned
1   gallon water
1   tablespoon salt
3   tablespoons Chili Sauce (see page 16)

$\mathcal{B}$ring water and salt to a boil. Add green beans and cook 5 to 10 minutes until tender.

Strain, toss with chili sauce, and serve immediately.

This is good the next day served cold.

SUMMER GREEN BEANS WITH HERBS

You can really only make this with very fresh tender beans. So many beans grow tough and stringy.
My test is to eat a few raw. If they're good like that, they'll be great like this.

{ SERVES 6. }

2½ pounds green beans
  1 gallon water
  1 tablespoon salt
  1 tablespoon butter
  ½ teaspoon white pepper
  4 leaves sorrel, cut in strips (optional)
  4 leaves mint, cut in strips
  1 tablespoon minced chives (or scallions)
     Juice of 1 lemon

Rinse the beans and string, if necessary. Trim off the stem end, and the tip end, if desired. Prepare a large bowl of ice water. Bring 1 gallon of water to a boil with the salt and drop in the beans. Cook uncovered to desired state of doneness (I cook mine about 3 minutes). Drain the beans and plunge into ice water to stop the cooking and preserve the color.

Melt the butter in the same pan. Drain the beans again and add to the pan, along with the minced herbs, lemon juice, pepper, and additional salt, if necessary. Toss the beans in the pan to coat evenly with the herb butter. Heat through and serve.

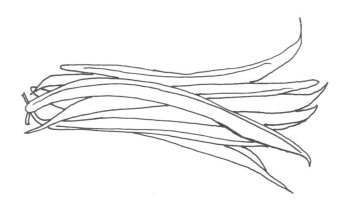

BUTTER BEANS

You'll have to ask him yourself, but I believe that this is my father's favorite vegetable ever.
He buys bushels of them in the summer, shucks them himself, and freezes them, so he can have good butter beans
all winter. Last June he still had some left from the summer before that hadn't been used up during the winter.
Still, his eyes shone brightly when he told me that the fresh beans would be ready the following week,
like a child at Christmas.

This is how Daddy cooks butter beans.

{ SERVES 4 TO 6. }

2   pounds baby limas or butter beans
4   to 5 cups water, to cover the beans generously
1   teaspoon salt
¼   cup butter

Rinse the beans well. Bring the water to boil with the salt and butter. Add the beans and bring back to a boil. Reduce heat to medium and cook the beans for about 30 minutes. Serve hot.

WHITE BEANS

We serve these at Martha's year-round, but especially love them in the winter.
With some chopped onion and hot water corn bread, it's all the meal I need!

{ SERVES ABOUT 6. }

1   pound dried great northern beans
     Country ham hock, tied in cheesecloth
     Water to cover the beans
1   beer
2   teaspoons salt
     Dash white vinegar

Rinse and sort the beans, place in a large bowl and cover with water by twice their volume. Refrigerate overnight. Drain and rinse the beans. Place in a heavy stock pot, cover again with water by twice their volume, add the ham hock, and bring to a boil.

Remove the scum that rises to the top, reduce the heat to low and cook, stirring occasionally, until the beans are tender, about 2 hours.

Add the beer, vinegar, and salt to taste and cook 20 minutes more. Remove from heat. Remove the ham hock and let cool until easily handled. Pull away any meat from the hock, place the meat back in the pot, and stir well. Serve with raw chopped onion, pepper vinegar sauce, and corn bread to sop up the juice.

As Grandpa said on *Hee Haw,* "Yum, Yum!"

OCTOBER BEANS

October beans are available along with the other fresh peas during those precious weeks of July.
You wish you could spread out the bounty a little. I just find myself cooking peas and beans every day
for several weeks. No one at home has complained yet.

Octobers get nice and soupy when you cook them down with a little pork. Perfect with corn bread.
Look in the soups and salads sections for other ideas for October beans.

{ SERVES 8. }

2 pounds October beans
1 thick slice fat back or slab bacon, or a little trimming from country ham
½ onion, chopped
1 cayenne pepper, dried or fresh, left whole

Rinse the beans and set aside. Place the pork in a large pot with about 2 quarts of water. Bring to a boil and stir in the beans and onion and the pepper. Add more water if needed to cover the beans by at least 3 inches. Bring back to a boil, skim any scum that comes to the top, and turn the beans down to medium. Cook the beans about 20 minutes until tender. Taste the beans and season with salt, if needed. Remember, the pork is very salty. Let the beans cook down until some fall apart and the liquid gets soupy. Add more water if they get too dry. Serve with corn bread.

CROWDER PEA AND CABBAGE STEW

Crowder peas look like black-eyes, but their eyes aren't black. To me, they taste a little "greener" than black-eyes. Crowders can be cooked just like fresh limas or black-eyes. Vary the time depending on the freshness and size of the pea. Here's a summer stew featuring crowders.

{ SERVES 6. }

1	pound crowders (fresh or frozen)
	Water to cover
3	cloves garlic, peeled
2	bay leaves
2	teaspoons salt
	Dash cayenne pepper
	Dash white pepper
1	tablespoon olive oil
1	onion, chopped
½	head green cabbage, roughly chopped
2	to 3 large fresh tomatoes, chopped
1	quart water
2	teaspoons salt
	Black pepper to taste
½	can beer
½	bunch fresh parsley
4	scallions, thinly sliced

Rinse the crowders, place in a heavy pot, and cover by 2 inches with cold water. Add the garlic cloves, bay leaves, salt, cayenne, and white pepper and bring to a boil. Skim the foam that rises up, stir the peas, turn down the heat a little, and cook until they're just tender. Drain, reserving the garlic and bay leaves.

Place the pot back on the stove and heat the olive oil. Add the onion and cook on high for about 4 minutes. Meanwhile, mince the reserved cooked garlic cloves and add to the pot. Add the cabbage and cook on high for about 3 or 4 minutes. Stir in the crowders along with the bay leaves and the chopped tomatoes. Cook about 3 minutes, stirring. Add the water and the additional salt and pepper. Bring to a boil. Stir, reduce the heat to medium, and cook, stirring occasionally, for about 15 minutes. Add the beer and cook 10 more minutes. Add the parsley and scallions, and continue to cook. You want the crowders tender, but not falling apart. The sauce should be somewhat thickened.

Taste and adjust the seasoning. Discard the bay leaves. Serve as a side, or as a meal over a bowl of rice or mashed potatoes.

BLACK–EYED PEAS (HOPPIN' JOHN)

You must have these on New Year's Day. A whole year's luck depends upon it, and a whole day's eating satisfaction.

{ SERVES 6 TO 8. }

1　pound fresh or dried black-eyed peas
2　tablespoons butter
1　yellow onion, diced
2　stalks celery, diced
1　green bell pepper, diced
2½　quarts chicken stock
1　tablespoon salt
1　teaspoon black pepper
2　dried cayenne peppers
1　bay leaf
1　cup long grain rice
½　yellow onion, diced
　　Hot sauce

If using dried peas (which you will be doing in January, in this hemisphere at least) rinse and sort, and soak overnight in water. If using fresh, rinse and sort through. Set aside. Melt the butter in a heavy soup stock pot and cook the onion, celery, and bell pepper just to wilt. Add the stock and bring to a boil. Add the peas, salt, pepper, cayenne, and bay leaf. Return to a boil and skim any scum that rises to the top. Reduce the heat to medium low and cook until the peas are just tender, about 1 hour for dried peas and 15 minutes for fresh.

Add the rice and stir well. Add water to cover by about 1 inch. Cover and cook for 15 more minutes, or until the rice is done and the stock is absorbed. Discard the bay leaf.

Serve with raw chopped onion and vinegar hot sauce such as Crystal or Red Rooster.

BRUSSELS SPROUTS WITH BROWN BUTTER

I crave these in the fall. They go great with roasted turkey or flavorful game like rabbit.

{ SERVES 6 TO 8. }

2   pounds fresh Brussels sprouts
2   quarts water
2   teaspoons salt
¼   cup butter
2   scallions, thinly sliced
    Zest and juice of 1 lemon
    Salt and white pepper to taste

Trim the ends of the Brussels sprouts and cut in half lengthwise. Pour the water into a saucepan and bring to a boil with the salt. Add the Brussel sprouts and cook until tender but not mushy, about 7 minutes. Drain the Brussels sprouts.

Heat the butter in a heavy skillet and add the sprouts and scallions, tossing to coat. Carefully allow the butter to brown, not burn. Add the lemon juice, zest, and salt and pepper as desired. Serve immediately.

BOILED CABBAGE WITH BUTTER

I really, really love this cabbage. It's probably my ultimate comfort food. I think I like boiled cabbage best on crisp evenings in early spring when my senses demand something green that will still warm my bones.
I almost always serve it with Garlic Mashed Potatoes (see page 130).
In fact, I'm divinely happy with a big soup bowl filled with just those two.

{ SERVES 10. }

1   head green cabbage
3   quarts water
¼   cup butter
1   tablespoon salt
1   teaspoon cracked black pepper
1   pod dried cayenne pepper
    Juice of 2 lemons

C ore the cabbage and roughly chop. Place in a pot and cover with water. Add butter, salt, and peppers, and bring to a boil. Reduce the heat and cook on low about 15 or so minutes until cooked but still slightly firm. Add lemon juice, adjust the seasonings, and serve.

BRAISED RED CABBAGE

I love this with fried pork chops or sausages. A great cold-weather vegetable.

{ SERVES 10. }

- 1　head red cabbage
- 1　small red onion, thinly sliced
- 1　tablespoon vegetable oil
- ½　cup red wine
- ¼　cup red wine vinegar
- 1　tablespoon firmly packed brown sugar
- 1　teaspoon juniper berries (optional)
- 1　teaspoon salt
- ½　teaspoon white pepper
- ½　teaspoon celery seeds

C ore the cabbage and slice thinly. Heat the oil in a deep skillet or Dutch oven. Add the onion and sauté over fairly high heat until the onion is translucent. Add the cabbage and toss to coat well with the oil. Sauté until the cabbage is wilted. Add the wine, vinegar, brown sugar, juniper berries, salt, and pepper. Stir well and cover. Turn the heat to low and cook for about 15 to 20 minutes. Remove from the heat and stir in the celery seeds.

　　This is a marvelous bed for pork chops or rabbit, or even venison roasts.

STUFFED CABBAGE

There are a million ways to stuff cabbage. My favorite, and I believe the most traditional Southern way, is with rice and pork sausage. This is a most satisfying supper on a blustery winter's eve.

{ MAKES ABOUT 12 STUFFED CABBAGE LEAVES. }

1	head green cabbage, cored
2	quarts salted water
½	pound loose pork sausage
1	onion, finely diced
3	cloves garlic, minced
2	ribs celery, finely diced
1	carrot, finely diced
2	cups raw white rice
3	cups chicken stock
1	teaspoon red pepper flakes
1	bay leaf
1	teaspoon fresh sage, minced
1	teaspoon fresh thyme leaves
2	scallions, thinly sliced
1	tablespoon fresh chopped parsley
	Salt, if needed (the sausage is quite salty)
2	cups chicken stock

Remove and separate the large individual cabbage leaves. Bring the water to a simmer in a wide shallow pot and drop the cabbage leaves in until they wilt and become pliable, about 5 minutes. Drain on paper towels.

Cook the sausage in a deep skillet, breaking up the meat as it cooks. When the sausage is about halfway done add the onion, garlic, and celery, and cook with the sausage for about 5 minutes. Add the carrot and continue cooking a couple of minutes. Stir in the raw rice and cook for 2 minutes. Add 3 cups of stock, bring to a boil, and reduce to simmer. Add the pepper flakes and bay leaf. Cover and cook for about 10 minutes, until rice is about two thirds done. Remove from the heat and cool. Stir in the fresh herbs and adjust the seasoning.

Preheat the oven to 400°. Remove any very thick ribs from the cabbage leaves. Lay the cabbage leaves flat and, depending on the leaf size, place about 2 or 3 tablespoons of filling one third of the way up the center of the leaf. Roll the bottom third over the filling, fold over the sides, and roll up, not too tight. Fill remaining leaves in the same manner. Place the stuffed leaves in a Dutch oven and pour the remaining 2 cups of stock over. Cover the Dutch oven with a lid and bake for 20 to 30 minutes, until the rice is completely done. Serve with a little rich Tomato Sauce (see page 159).

COPPER PENNY CARROTS

These look very pretty on a plate in the winter when the vegetables tend to not inspire.

{ SERVES 6. }

2   quarts water
2   teaspoons salt
1   pound young carrots, peeled and sliced in thin coins
½   yellow onion, sliced in thin circles
3   tablespoons butter
¼   cup firmly packed brown sugar
1   teaspoon chopped fresh parsley

Bring the water to a boil with the salt. Add the remaining ingredients except the parsley. Turn the heat to medium and allow the liquid to reduce as the carrots cook. Watch so that they don't cook too quickly and scorch. Add a little more water if necessary. When the carrots are cooked, the liquid, butter, and sugar should be cooked down to a syrupy glaze. Sprinkle with chopped parsley and serve.

MACARONI AND CHEESE

Catherine Couch, my grandmother's housekeeper, made the best in the world, heavy on the black pepper.
I always got in trouble for picking off the crispy pieces on top.

{ SERVES 6. }

1   tablespoon salt
1   pound large shell pasta or rigatoni
1   tablespoon butter
2   eggs
1½ cups milk (or cream)
1   teaspoon ground black pepper
12 ounces sharp white Cheddar cheese, grated
    Paprika

Preheat the oven to 365°. Fill a large pot with water and the tablespoon of salt and bring to a boil. Pour in the pasta, stirring, and cook about 6 minutes, until slightly undercooked. Drain and run under cold water.

Place the pasta in a 2-quart casserole and toss with the butter to keep it from sticking. Beat together the eggs, milk or cream, and pepper, and pour over the pasta. Add three-fourths of the cheese and mix together. Sprinkle the rest of the cheese on top and then the paprika. Cover with foil and bake for 30 minutes.

Remove the foil and turn the broiler on to brown the top. Lightly brown and serve before someone, usually me, steals all of the browned pieces from the top.

BAKED CHEESE GRITS

{ SERVES 6. }

1   cup water
1   cup half and half
1   cup grits (preferably stone ground – not instant!)
    Salt and white pepper to taste
2/3 cup buttermilk
3   eggs, beaten
1   cup freshly grated parmesan

Preheat the oven to 350°.

In a saucepan bring the water and half and half to a boil with salt and white pepper. Whisk in the grits and cook until thickened. Pour into a mixing bowl.

In a separate bowl whisk together the buttermilk and eggs, and stir into the grits. Stir in the Parmesan. Pour the mixture into a greased casserole and bake for 30 minutes.

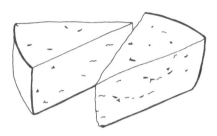

CHEESE SOUFFLÉ

This makes a very nice luncheon or light supper with a spinach salad and some fruit. You could get some really different flavors by varying the type of cheese. Cheddar is about all that's been around for the last several decades, and a good sharp Cheddar works great, but a goat cheese or something aged or Swiss or even blue would make it an entirely different dish.

{ SERVES 6 TO 8. }

2 tablespoons butter
2 tablespoons all-purpose flour
1 cup milk
  Dash white pepper
  Dash red pepper
1½ cups grated or crumbled cheese
3 eggs, separated

Preheat the oven to 300°. Grease a soufflé dish or casserole. Place butter in the top of a double boiler and melt over simmering water. Stir in the flour and cook a few minutes, and then add the milk and peppers. Cook for several minutes, then stir in the grated cheese. Beat the egg yolks and stir in. Let cook until thickened. Remove from the heat and let cool slightly. Beat the egg whites stiff and fold in. Spoon into the casserole and bake for 30 minutes, until risen and lightly browned.

CORN PUDDING WITH SAGE

I love the fresh sage with the corn and cheese. It makes this a really rich tasting dish. I don't recommend using dried sage. Sage is a semi-evergreen, and my sage stays green for a good ten months a year. It's very easy to grow and gets huge in a couple of years. Its pretty purple flowers make a great garnish, too.

{ SERVES 6. }

4   ears corn
1   tablespoon butter
½   yellow onion, diced
½   green bell pepper, diced
1   teaspoon salt
¼   teaspoon cayenne pepper
½   teaspoon black pepper
¼   cup cornmeal
2½ cups milk
2   eggs, beaten
2   teaspoons fresh sage, minced
½   cup Parmesan or other hard cheese, grated

Chuck and clean the corn and remove the kernels from the cob, scraping to remove milky liquid from the cob. Set the kernels with the liquid aside. Heat the butter in a deep skillet and sauté the onion for 3 minutes. Add the bell pepper and cook for 5 more minutes. Add the seasoning and cornmeal, and stir. Add the milk, stirring. Let the mixture cook 5 minutes, until thickened. Mix in the corn and liquid. Remove the skillet from the heat and stir in the beaten eggs, sage, and all but 2 tablespoons of the cheese. Pour the mixture into a casserole.

Make a steam bath by setting the casserole inside a slightly larger pan, filled halfway with hot water. Bake at 350° until the pudding is almost set, about 35 minutes.

Sprinkle with the remaining 2 tablespoons of cheese and cook for another 10 or so minutes until firm and browned on top. Serve hot.

FRIED CORN

*Fried corn as known in Middle Tennessee is not actually fried, but rather stewed with butter or bacon grease
and its own milky liquid. Daddy is a master at fried corn. He's liberal with the black pepper, and he can wait
to stir the corn until just the right moment when you get some yummy, chewy kind of crusty thing going on
underneath. Daddy and I both much prefer tougher field corn to the tender and sweeter Silver Queen
for this particular dish. Field corn has a nice toothsomeness to it and furthermore, Silver Queen is
sometimes just too blame sweet for me.*

{ SERVES 8. }

8   ears field corn
½   to 1 cup milk, if needed
¼   cup butter (or 3 tablespoons bacon grease)
2   teaspoons salt
1   teaspoon fresh ground black pepper

Chuck and clean the corn and cut the kernels from the cob. Use your knife to scrape
down the cob, milking it of all of its juice. If the corn doesn't have much milk, you may
put the corn in a bowl, pouring about a half cup of true milk over it. Heat the fat in a
cast-iron skillet. Add the corn with the milk, salt, and pepper. Stir once and let the corn
sit on medium high heat for several minutes before stirring or turning again. If the mixture seems too dry, add a little more milk, but you don't want it too runny, either. Turn
the heat down to low and let it cook, stirring occasionally, for about 20 minutes.

ROASTED OR GRILLED CORN

This cooking method really intensifies the rich sweet flavor of corn, and the grilled version adds a nice smokiness.

{ SERVES 6. }

6   ears corn
½   cup butter, softened
     Salt and pepper to taste

Preheat the oven to 425° or light the grill. Pull the shucks down from the corn cobs,
not removing them. Remove the the silks. Spread a teaspoon or two of the butter over
the corn kernels and sprinkle with salt and pepper if desired. Pull the shucks back up
over the ears and tie with twine to secure. Place the ears of corn on indirect heat on
the grill or directly onto the racks of the oven and cook, turning occasionally on the grill
for 30 minutes. Remove the husks and serve with additional butter and seasoning.

Grits

*M*any old cookbooks refer to grits as hominy. If you look at a package of grits close-ly, you'll see that most actually say "hominy grits." Hominy refers to the fact that the corn is dried and hulled (the outside of the kernel removed). Grits are then ground.

To my fancy cosmopolitan friends, I explain that grits are simply polenta, the trendy Italian corn-mash generally made with white corn instead of yellow. Like polenta, grits are incredibly versatile. They can be cooked stove top and served creamy, usually the way you have them for breakfast with your eggs. You can also mix them with seasoning and cheese and bake them, or you can spread the hot grits in a shallow baking dish, chill it, cut out the grits in shapes and pan fry it.

Like all cereals, creamy grits need to be highly seasoned to taste worth a damn. To most Southerners this means salt, black pepper, and maybe a little hot sauce, plus plenty of butter. Then, of course, you scrape your bacon or country ham in them, break in your fried egg, and kind of mush the whole thing around a bit in your own personal style. This is actually what makes grits taste good. I have known those who ate sweet-ened grits as you would cream of wheat, but you don't see it too often and I can't say I recommend the practice.

SIMPLE GRITS

{ Serves 4. }

4   cups water
1   teaspoon salt
1   cup grits (not quick cooking if you can possibly help it)
1   tablespoon butter (or more)

*B*ring the salted water to boil in a saucepan and stir in the grits. Turn the heat down to medium and cook the grits, stirring until very thick, about 20 minutes. Serve with butter, salt, and pepper.

Grits marked "quick grits" are a lot like quick oatmeal. They take about 10 minutes less time and seem to be something that a lot of us have gotten used to. A tasting of the slow-cooking variety (preferably from a small operation such as Nora Mill in north-ern Georgia) will remind you of how grits are supposed to taste.

SEASONED HOMINY

Hominy is corn that has had the hull removed. Rather a strange idea, particularly when you realize that lye is used in the processing. Regardless, hominy is a mainstay in Southern and in Mexican cooking.
Grits are actually ground from hominy. Canned hominy is a wonderful and inexpensive addition to stews and soups, or a very tasty side dish with just a little jazzing up.

{ SERVES 4. }

1   28-ounce can white hominy
1   tablespoon olive oil
½   yellow onion, diced
3   cloves garlic, minced
2   ripe tomatoes, diced
1   teaspoon salt
¼   teaspoon cayenne pepper
¼   teaspoon paprika
¼   teaspoon black pepper
    Juice of ½ lemon

Drain and rinse the hominy. Set aside. Heat the oil in a skillet. Add the onion and cook 3 minutes. Add the garlic and cook 1 more minute. Add the tomatoes, salt, and peppers, and stir. Let cook about 10 minutes, until the tomatoes are beginning to dry out. Add the hominy to the pan and cook just to heat through, about 5 minutes. Stir in the lemon juice and serve.

SAUTÉED CUCUMBER

The trick to cooking cucumbers is to cook them lightly or the texture becomes ugly and the flavor nonexistent. I think perhaps that this concept of light application is difficult for us who were raised with mainly bland vegetables picked under-ripe and shipped across country. We're so used to adding lots of seasoning or heavy sauces in an attempt to give flavor to the flavorless that it's hard for us to allow a beautiful, simple thing to be simply beautiful. My goodness, such a sermon.

{ S E R V E S 4. }

2   teaspoons butter
2   very fresh cucumbers, sliced
1   teaspoon minced chervil or tarragon
    Dash salt and white pepper
    Juice of ¼ lemon

Warm the butter in a skillet to just sizzling and toss in the cucumber, shaking the pan to coat the slices. Cook quickly on high heat for 3 or 4 minutes, until the cucumbers are heated through and slightly wilted. Add the remaining ingredients, toss well, and serve immediately.

Eggplant

Eggplant is another vegetable that lingered near obscurity in the South for the greater part of this century. My parents claim that they ate eggplant as children, but my first impression of eggplant was of some exotic, threateningly obscene novelty which I would see at the County Fair. The only thing I could figure out that people did with eggplant was to try to grow the biggest one and win a blue ribbon from 4H. My real romance with eggplant began in my late teens and hasn't faltered yet. Some day I would love to write an entire book extolling the virtues of eggplant, so I won't risk boring you here. Just let me say that eggplant is as happy to be in the South as Southerners are happy to eat it. Eggplant does phenomenally well in our hot and humid summers. It's the perfect vegetable for a novice gardener to plant, or a good one to find at farmers' markets and vegetable stands. Look for some heirloom varieties that are different colors and shapes.

STEWED EGGPLANT

This is a lot like the Provençal dish ratatouille. We serve it at Martha's during the summer.

{ SERVES 8. }

¼ cup olive oil
1 yellow onion, diced medium
1 eggplant, the skin scored and diced large
1 green bell pepper, chopped
1 red bell pepper, chopped
1 pint mushrooms, quartered (optional)
4 ripe tomatoes, peeled and roughly chopped
5 cloves garlic, minced
2 tablespoons red wine vinegar
1 teaspoon fresh thyme leaves
1 teaspoon summer savory (optional)
1 tablespoon salt
2 teaspoons black pepper
½ teaspoon red pepper flakes

Heat the oil in a Dutch oven. Add the onion and cook 5 minutes. Add the eggplant and cook 5 more minutes. Add the peppers, garlic, and mushrooms, and cook 5 minutes. Add the tomatoes and cook 5 more minutes. Add the remaining ingredients and cook over medium for 20 to 30 minutes.

My grandmother served this as one of the many vegetable dishes that appeared on the dinner table. Stewed eggplant is great over rice or pasta or pour it into a casserole, top with breadcrumbs and a little fresh goat cheese, and bake. Serve as a main dish with a salad and some bread.

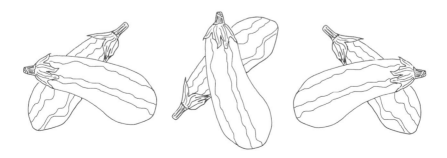

EGGPLANT "FRIES"

Eggplant is so good like this. Crispy coating and smooth and savory inside.
Serve it with fresh lemon, or maybe a little tomato sauce.

The only problem I have with this recipe is that I have a tendency to eat most of the eggplant before I can
get it to the table. Consider doubling the recipe.

{ S E R V E S   6 . }

1	large eggplant
3	eggs
¾	cup dry breadcrumbs
¼	teaspoon cayenne pepper
¼	teaspoon black pepper
¼	teaspoon garlic powder
½	teaspoon dried oregano
½	cup vegetable oil
	Salt to taste

Peel the eggplant and cut into finger-size pieces. Sprinkle heavily with salt and place in a colander to drain for 1 hour. This rids the eggplant of any bitter juices. Press lightly on the eggplant to drain. Beat the eggs. Mix the breadcrumbs with the seasonings and place in a plate. Drop the eggplant fingers in the egg and roll each in the bread crumbs to coat. Place coated fingers on a baking sheet and place in the freezer for 15 minutes. This makes the breading adhere.

In a deep skillet heat the oil to 325° or almost smoking. Fry the chilled eggplant fingers a few at a time until browned on all sides. Drain on clean brown paper bags. Sprinkle with salt and serve hot. They're great dipped in a simple Tomato Sauce (see page 159).

MARINATED SUMMER VEGETABLES

{ SERVES 8. }

1   medium eggplant, cut in ½-inch rounds
1   zucchini, cut in ½-inch rounds
2   red bell peppers, cut in ½-inch rings
     Salt and pepper
1   red onion, cut into ½-inch rings
5   cloves garlic, minced
     Olive oil
2   tablespoons red wine vinegar

Preheat the grill to medium.

Sprinkle the sliced vegetables with salt and pepper. Grill in batches until quite tender and a little toasty, turning once or twice (about 5 minutes per side). Place whole slices of onion on the grill and try to turn in one piece, grilling about 5 minutes per side. Combine all of the vegetables in a large mixing bowl with the garlic, red wine vinegar, and basil. Serve warm or at room temperature.

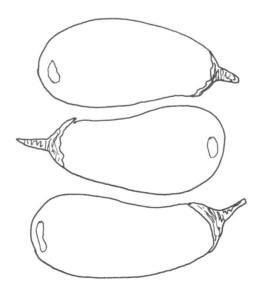

Greens

ℋooray for greens! Let them be heralded among the noble vegetables and in the voices and hearts of man! Greens are one of the foods for which my body physically yearns and aches. When I was pregnant and bordering on anemia, I practically ate my weight in greens: turnips, mustard, collards, kale, and an occasional bowl of poke salet. Greens to me taste like life itself, pungent, vibrant, and and full of pepper. I especially love greens in the cool months of spring when I need a tonic from the winter and again in autumn when my blood begins to race with the prospect of first frost. These are the best seasons for greens, the shoots are young and tender and the flavor more teasing than it is bold.

Other than poke salet, which is in a class all its own, I have two ways of cooking all varieties of greens. The first is purely traditional with salty ham and pepper. My own "newfangled" recipe for greens upsets purists like my father, until they take their first bite. I haven't missed a convert yet.

OLD–FASHIONED GREENS

In tough times, this would be the extent of many Southern suppers, along with some corn bread to mop up the "licker." I'm sure it made tough times a little less tough. Now it is usually one of several vegetables offered with dinner. Hot sauce would be greatly appreciated with this fine dish.

{ S E R V E S 8 . }

4   bunches greens (kale, collard, mustard, turnip, or dandelion)
½   pound country ham trimmings (or a meaty bone)
4   or more dried whole cayennes
1   gallon water
1   to 2 teaspoons salt, or to taste

Pick the greens well, removing the tough stems, and wash very well in a couple or even several changes of cold water, if necessary. Fill a large pot with water and add the ham hock. Bring to a boil and cook for 20 minutes before adding the greens and salt. Remember, the pork is already salty. Bring back to a boil, reduce the heat, and cook until quite tender, an hour or more.

Note: Some people like to soak their dandelion greens in ice water for an hour before cooking to remove some of the bitterness. Picking only the youngest greens will avoid this problem.

GREENS WITH TOMATOES

{ S ERVES 6. }

2   bunches greens
¼   cup olive oil
1   yellow or white onion, thinly sliced
3   cloves garlic, minced
1   25-ounce can tomatoes
2   cups plus water
    Salt to taste (start with 1½ teaspoons)
    Black pepper to taste
    Several squirts hot sauce
1   tablespoon malt vinegar

Clean the greens well and wash in several changes of cold water, as necessary. Drain. Heat the oil in a stock pot and sauté the onion and garlic. Toss in the greens and stir until wilted. Add the tomatoes and their juice, squeezing the tomatoes to break them up. Add the remaining ingredients and bring to a boil. Reduce the heat to medium and cook for 45 or so minutes, until the greens are tender but not mushy. You may need to add a little water. Adjust the seasoning to taste. Serve with corn bread and additional hot sauce and vinegar. This will clean your insides out and wake the sleepiest of taste buds.

POKE SALET

Poke salet is very rarely seen in the grocery store, but it is seen in every yard in which I have ever mucked about in Middle Tennessee. The berries of the plant are poisonous, and even the leaves really must be long cooked or they'll upset most stomachs. If the plant gets too large, the greens will be frighteningly bitter, but the young leaves are simply, shall we say, pronounced in flavor.

Clean the greens well and cook as in the above old-fashioned greens recipe, with maybe a little less water. When the greens are done, after a couple of hours, drain off about 2 cups. Heat a little bacon fat in a skillet. Stir in the greens and 3 beaten eggs. Scramble together.

This is a feast served with Hot Water Corn Bread (see page 216) and a vinegar pepper sauce.

SPICY KALE

{ SERVES 8. }

¼   c olive oil
1   red onions, sliced radially
4   quarts kale, trimmed and rinsed
2   teaspoons salt
1   tablespoon minced fresh garlic
2   tablespoons red wine vinegar
1   16-ounce can tomatoes with juice
1   tomato can water
1   tablespoon hot sauce
1   beer

*I*n a rondeau heat the oil. Add the onions and cook for 5 minutes. Add the kale and salt. Wilt the kale, stirring frequently. Add the remaining ingredients. Bring to a boil. Reduce the heat and simmer for 40 minutes, stirring occasionally. Taste and adjust the seasonings if necessary.

WILTED SPINACH

{ SERVES 4. }

3   tablespoons olive oil
½   red onion, thinly sliced
2   garlic cloves, minced
1   pound cleaned spinach leaves
½   teaspoon salt
    Juice of ½ lemon

*I*n a deep skillet heat the olive oil over medium high heat. Add the onion and cook about 2 minutes. Add the spinach, garlic, and the salt. Toss and cook about 2 more minutes, until the spinach is wilted. Add the lemon juice and toss. Serve immediately.

SPINACH SOUFFLÉ

{ SERVES 4. }

½ pound fresh spinch, cleaned and chopped
1 teaspoon plus ½ teaspoon salt
5 tablespoons butter
7 tablespoons all-purpose flour
1 cup milk
   Salt to taste
2½ teaspoons white pepper
   Nutmeg to taste
7 eggs, separated
5 scallions, chopped

Sprinkle the spinach with salt and place in a strainer. Let drain for 1 hour.

In a small pot melt the butter. Add the flour, stirring constantly to a smooth paste. Add the hot milk and stir to make a thick sauce. Add a little salt, pepper, and nutmeg. Remove from the heat. Add the spinach and scallions to the sauce.

Preheat the oven to 350°. Beat the egg yolks until very thick. In a separate bowl beat the whites until stiff. Fold the yolks into the sauce, then fold in the whites. Pour into buttered mold.

Bake for about 30 minutes, until the soufflé puffs and is lightly browned. Serve immediately.

Okra

Okra is a sacred vegetable in the South and throughout the Caribbean. Africans brought okra seeds with them across the ocean on the heinous slave ships. A seed of hope and life amongst so much horror.

Okra grows like a weed in our hot and muggy summers. The only difficulty with growing okra here is catching the vegetable while it is still small and tender. They mature very quickly becoming woody and tough. Do yourself and your friends a favor and only prepare small okra, even for frying and stews. The smallest ones are delightful fried whole.

FRIED OKRA

{ SERVES 4. }

1   cup cornmeal
½   teaspoon garlic powder
½   teaspoon salt
¼   teaspoon cayenne pepper
¼   teaspoon black pepper
1   cup buttermilk
1   pound okra, cut in ½-inch slices (leave smaller okra whole)
½   cup vegetable oil

Mix the dry ingredients in a bowl. Pour the buttermilk into another bowl. Clean and prep the okra and place in the buttermilk. Lift the okra from the buttermilk with a slotted spoon and roll in the cornmeal mixture. When the pieces are well covered, place them on a plate or baking sheet and put in the freezer for 15 minutes to set the coating. Heat the oil in an iron skillet to 325° or just below smoking. Add the okra to the hot oil and cook for 5 to 7 minutes, turning to brown on all sides. Drain on paper towels, sprinkle with salt, and serve hot.

STEWED OKRA

Tastes like the glories of summer. I can't get enough.

{ SERVES 6. }

¼   cup olive oil

1   yellow onion, diced medium

3   cloves garlic, minced

1   or 2 banana peppers,cut in ½-inch slices

1   pound okra (leave small okra whole, otherwise cut into ½- or 1-inch slices)

½   pound small tender okra, stem ends trimmed

1   teaspoon salt

1   teaspoon black pepper

¼   teaspoon red pepper flakes (optional)

2   fresh tomatoes, peeled (optional) and roughly chopped

2   tablespoons red wine vinegar

2   scallions, sliced (optional)

Heat the oil in a heavy skillet and sauté the onion for 3 minutes. Add the garlic and peppers and cook 2 more minutes. Add the okra, salt, and peppers, and cook 5 minutes. Add the tomato and cook on medium high for about 5 minutes, until a little dry. Add the vinegar and cook another 5 minutes. Stir, reduce the heat to low, and cook another 5 or 10 minutes, until the okra is very tender. Sprinkle with sliced scallions, if you like, and serve hot. This is a meal over rice, or just one of the many vegetable dishes to laden a Southern dinner table.

I have heard some misguided souls complain about the "slimy texture" of okra. I myself find the texture more luxurious than slimy, however I will note that leaving the okra whole will hold in most of its juices, greatly alleviating the "slime factor."

SCALLOPED ONIONS

Rich and savory, serve them with a simple roast.

{ SERVES 6 TO 8. }

6   yellow onions (Vidalia, if in season)
    Water
2   teaspoons salt
1   cup breadcrumbs
½   tablespoon salt
¼   teaspoon black pepper
2   teaspoons fresh thyme leaves
1   cup butter
1   cup heavy cream
¼   cup Parmesan cheese

Preheat the oven to 350°. Slice the onions about 1-inch thick. Place in a heavy pot with about 1 inch of water to cover them. Add the salt and bring to a boil. Cover, reduce the heat to low, and cook for 15 minutes or so until the onions are tender. Add a little more water, if necessary, to keep the onions covered.

Drain the onions and place in a baking dish, layering with a sprinkle of bread-crumbs, a little salt and pepper, and thyme, and dotting with pieces of butter. Place the last layer of onions and pour the cream over. Top with breadcrumbs and Parmesan, and bake for 30 to 40 minutes until bubbly and browned on top.

GLAZED ONIONS

Wonderful with a hundred dishes. The perfect "sauce" for simply grilled meat, the classic with fried calf's liver.
This makes an awesome "bed" for grilled fish or chicken or an intriguing topping for a green salad.

{ SERVES 6. }

3   yellow onions
¼   cup butter
1   tablespoon firmly packed brown sugar
2   teaspoons salt
½   teaspoon white pepper
¼   cup red wine vinegar

Thinly slice the onions. Heat the butter in a cast-iron skillet and add the brown sugar, stirring to dissolve. Add the onions with the salt and pepper, stirring. Cook the onions on medium high until they are translucent. Turn the heat to low and cook slowly for 1 hour or so, stirring occasionally to avoid burning. Turn heat back to high and, when the pan starts to sizzle, pour in the vinegar, stirring constantly. Cook for a few more minutes, until the vinegar is syrupy.

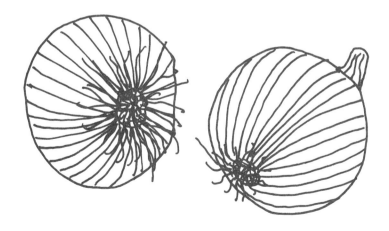

ONION SOUFFLÉ

A hearty tasting dish for a blustery, dark night.

{ S ERVES 6 TO 8 . }

¼   cup butter

4   large yellow onions, finely chopped

Salt to taste

½   teaspoon white pepper

2   teaspoons minced fresh sage

3   tablespoons all-purpose flour

1   cup milk

¼   cup grated cheese (something twangy like a fresh goat or yogurt cheese)

5   egg whites

½   teaspoon cream of tartar

*P*reheat the oven to 350°. Heat 2 tablespoons of the butter in a skillet and cook the onions on medium high until translucent. Reduce the heat and simmer on low, stirring occasionally, for about 15 minutes. Transfer the mixture to a food processor or blender and purée. Season with salt, pepper, and sage, and set aside. You should have about 2 cups.

Heat the remaining butter in a saucepan and stir in the flour to a smooth consistency. Cook on medium for about 5 minutes, stirring constantly.

Meanwhile, heat the milk slightly. Pour the milk into the roux, whisking out any lumps. Bring the sauce to a slight boil. Turn the heat to low and cook, stirring occasionally, for 10 minutes. Add the onion, stir well, and cook another 10 minutes. Add the cheese and stir until melted. Remove from the heat and let the mixture cool.

Beat the egg whites until almost stiff. Sprinkle the cream of tartar over the egg whites and continue to beat until stiff. Gently fold the egg whites into the onion mixture, careful not to over mix. Pour into a 3-quart soufflé dish and bake for about 30 minutes, until risen and browned on top. Serve immediately.

ONION RINGS

Who can resist? Crispy, sweet, and savory. And these are the best.

{ SERVES 6. }

4   yellow onions
1   cup all-purpose flour
1   tablespoon salt
1   teaspoon black pepper
3   cups buttermilk
4   cups vegetable oil
2   cups cornmeal
1   tablespoon salt
1   teaspoon cayenne pepper

Peel the onions and slice ½-inch thin. Place the flour in a large bowl. Stir the salt and black pepper in with the flour. Pour in the buttermilk and mix. Separate the onions into rings and drop into the batter. Refrigerate the batter with the onion rings in it for an hour.

Heat the oil to 325° or just under smoking. Place the cornmeal on a plate and stir in the salt and pepper. Lift the onion rings from the batter and dredge in the cornmeal before frying. Fry about 5 minutes, turning, until golden brown. Drain on clean paper bags, sprinkle with salt, and serve.

Parsnips

Oh, pity the poor parsnip. Once so highly regaled and fondly munched upon, now we can scarcely find the fellow in the grocery store. And, if you do find a parsnip, chances are very good that it will be encased in a thick wax coating to maximize its shelf life. Of course I have been told many times that the wax is not toxic and that you can chip the wax away. I say who wants wax of any form, toxic or non, coating their insides or mucking up their kitchen table and floor. Please, take a stand and tell your grocer that you simply don't want wax. Perhaps, if we all bend their ears, the farmers will hear and the parsnip may once again bask in its own naked beauty.

We must do our part by eating lots and lots of parsnips at a suitable rate of consumption so that they do not rot on the grocery store shelves. And what a delightful task. In case you're not familiar, a parsnip is carrot-like in shape and slightly turnip-like in taste. Parsnips become sweeter after the temperature drops to forty degrees for several hours or days, even, making them a cold weather vegetable. The texture when cooked may range from slightly firm to mashed and puréed. Parsnips add a new depth to stews or pot pies, and a wonderful twangy richness to mashed potatoes. Parsnip recipes were all over cook books from the last century, but like so many vegetables of character, were somehow streamlined out of vogue. I do see parsnips popping up in more cook's magazines and on trendy menus these days, so hopefully the parsnip's days of obscurity are numbered.

BUTTERED PARSNIPS

{ Serves 6. }

6 large parsnips
   Water to cover
2 teaspoons salt
1 teaspoon white pepper
1 bay leaf
1 tablespoon butter
1 tablespoon minced fresh parsley

*P*eel the parsnips and slice in discs, halving and quartering the discs as the parsnip widens, to get pieces of relatively the same size. Place the parsnips in a saucepan, cover with water, and add the salt, pepper, and bay leaf. Bring to a boil. Reduce the heat to medium and cook the parsnips until tender, about 10 minutes. Drain the parsnips, discard the bay leaf, and return to the pan along with the butter. Shake the pan until the butter is melted. Add the parsley and shake the pan to coat the parsnips. Check seasoning for salt and pepper and serve immediately.

SCALLOPED PARSNIPS

Very old cook books frequently call for bacon with parsnips. The smoky flavor is a satisfying match to the pungency of parsnips. Not many of us cook with bacon grease these days for numerous and obvious reasons. However, if you feel like throwing caution to wind, this is a good place to do so.

{ SERVES 6. }

1	tablespoon butter (or bacon grease)
½	yellow onion, thinly sliced
6	large parsnips
	Water to cover
2	teaspoons salt
½	cup shredded strong white Cheddar or blue cheese
½	cup cream
½	cup toasted breadcrumbs
1	tablespoon chopped fresh parsley
	Dash cayenne or paprika

Preheat the oven to 350°. Heat the butter or bacon grease in a skillet and cook the onions for about 5 minutes until translucent,. Peel the parsnips and cut lengthwise in 1/2-inch thick slices. Place the parsnips in a pot and cover with water. Add salt and bring to a boil. Reduce the heat to medium and barely cook through the parsnips, about 3 or 4 minutes. Drain the parsnips. Place half in a casserole, scattering half the onions over. Sprinkle about a fourth of the cheese over. Repeat with one more layer, and pour cream over. Sprinkle breadcrumbs and the remaining cheese on top. Top with a dash of cayenne or paprika. Cover with foil and bake for 20 minutes.

Remove the foil and place back in the oven for 10 more minutes. Sprinkle parsley over and serve hot.

ROASTED FALL VEGETABLES

{ Makes 3 quarts, about 8 to 10 servings. }

1   quart cauliflower florets
1   quart broccoli florets
3   to 4 parsnips, peeled, sliced 1-inch thick on the diagonal
4   carrots, peeled, cut 1-inch thick on the diagonal
3   beets, peeled, cut into uniform pieces
5   tablespoons olive oil
    Salt and black pepper

2   tablespoons red wine vinegar
1   tablespoon honey
1   teaspoon minced fresh garlic

Preheat the oven to 400°. Toss each item separately on baking sheets with 1 tablespoon olive oil, and a pinch of salt and pepper. Roast until tender, but still somewhat crisp. Allow to cool.

Blend all 5 veggies together in a large bowl.

Add the vinegar, honey, and garlic, and toss to coat. Serve warm or at room temperature.

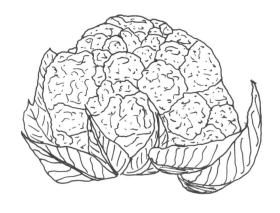

Peas

Fresh peas are a great luxury. It takes a lot of time to shell them, with a fairly low yield. Think of it as therapy. Shelling peas will force you to slow down. A rocking chair is nice place to sit while shelling and a front or back porch is a nice place for the rocking chair. A friend or relation is a nice person to shell with, but not a necessity. You'll probably find yourself humming a little tune if you shell alone. And what rewards! A fresh pea is an altogether different creature from the canned or frozen version. Fresh peas are as delicate and flirtatious as spring itself. Leave the processed peas for stews and pot pies. Fresh peas should be simply cooked.

FRESH PEAS WITH BUTTER AND MINT

Perhaps the best way to serve those little green pearls, so that the flavor can really shine through.

{ SERVES 6. }

4	cups fresh shelled peas
	Water to cover
2	teaspoons salt
½	teaspoon white pepper
¼	cup butter
1	tablespoon fresh mint, roughly chopped

Rinse and clean the peas. Place in a pot and cover with water. Add salt and pepper and bring to a boil. Reduce the heat to medium and cook about 10 to 15 minutes until the peas are tender but not mushy. Drain the peas and return to the pot with the butter, shaking the pan until the butter melts. Add mint and toss to coat. Serve immediately.

PEAS AND CARROTS WITH CREAM

A very pretty, delicate tasting spring vegetable. Lovely with roasted chicken or lamb.

{ SERVES 6. }

3 cups fresh shelled peas
2 carrots, diced
   Water to cover
2 teaspoons salt
1 teaspoon white pepper
1 bay leaf
1 pint cream
¼ onion, minced
1 tablespoon minced fresh dill

Rinse and clean the peas. Place in a pot with the diced carrots. Cover with water and add the salt, pepper, and bay leaf. Bring to a boil. Reduce the heat to medium high and cook about 10 minutes until tender. Drain. Meanwhile, pour the cream into a saucepan with the onion and bring to a simmer. Simmer until the cream is reduced by half. Place the peas and carrots back in the saucepan and add the reduced cream. Stir and place on the stove until the vegetables are heated. Stir in the dill and serve immediately.

CREOLE SHRIMP–STUFFED PEPPERS

A beautiful entrée you can make in advance. Serve them with rich Tomato Sauce (see page 159).

{ SERVES 6 AS THE MAIN COURSE. }

6   large green bell peppers
3   tablespoons vegetable oil
½   yellow onion, diced
3   cloves garlic, minced
2   ribs celery, diced
½   red bell pepper, diced

1½ cups white rice
1   teaspoon salt
½   teaspoon black pepper
¼   teaspoon cayenne pepper
¼   teaspoon paprika
1   bay leaf
3   cups chicken or vegetable stock
1   pound small shrimp, shelled
1   teaspoon fresh minced rosemary
1   teaspoon minced fresh thyme
1   teaspoon minced fresh basil
1   tablespoon dry breadcrumbs
1   tablespoon minced fresh parsley
1   tablespoon minced scallions

Cut the tops off of the peppers and clean out the ribs and seeds from the inside. Bring a pot of salted water to boil and parboil the peppers about 3 minutes. Drain and reserve. Heat the oil in a deep skillet and cook the onion until translucent. Add the garlic, celery, and red bell pepper, and cook about 5 minutes. Add the rice and stir, cooking until rice is pearly looking. Add the salt, peppers, paprika, bay leaf, and stock. Bring to a boil, stirring well. Cover, reduce the heat, and simmer for 10 minutes. Remove the lid and lightly stir in the shrimp, fresh rosemary, thyme, and basil. Cover and continue cooking for 5 more minutes. Remove from the stove and let cool.

Preheat the oven to 375°. Taste the stuffing and adjust the seasoning to suit your taste. Generously fill each pepper with the stuffing (any leftover stuffing may be saved and used to stuff trout, squash, tomatoes, onions, mushrooms, or eggplant, or simply eaten on its own). Sprinkle the top of each pepper with breadcrumbs, then parsley and scallions. Bake uncovered for 20 minutes until heated through and brown on top.

Mashed Potatoes

I've done a lot of thinking about, experimenting with, talking about, and eating of mashed potatoes. I have a few strong opinions. First and foremost, let's discuss the type of potato you will be mashing. Bakers, or russets, those beautiful, large, almost flawless football shaped potatoes, are not the potatoes for mashing; the smaller, lumpier, and more irregular shaped potatoes are. These have less water and more flavor and sugar than standard bakers. There are several specific varieties I like, such as Yellow Finnish and Yukon Golds, which mash marvelously into mashed potatoes of body and flavor. Potatoes have such a long life after harvest that they suffer the least of all vegetables from great cross-country trucking adventures. However, almost every part of the country has its own potato crops, and, as with all produce, fresher local potatoes will inevitably taste the best. Plus, you can feel good about supporting local trade.

So now you have selected your potatoes and it's time to cook them. Stop! Don't peel those potatoes! Rinse them, scrub them if you must, but please don't peel them. Potato skins hold in the flavor, nutrients, and texture while the potatoes boil. If you peel a potato before you boil it in water the water will taste like potatoes and the potatoes will taste like water. Fine for potato soup but hardly the thing for rich and yummy mashed potatoes. Also, season the cooking water well. If you don't salt the water, you'll be playing catch-up with the cooked potato and actually have to use more salt. Essentially, when salt is added at the cooking stage it enhances the flavor of food. Salt added afterwards never truly permeates the food and you will always taste the salt.

These are my three golden rules of mashed potatoes: use a thin-skinned, waxy potato, local if you can find them; cook them with the peel on; heavily season the water with salt and a little pepper if you choose. From this point, there really are no rules. I've mashed potatoes with sun-dried tomatoes, blue cheese, and even roasted jalapeños. In keeping with the nature of this treatise, the following recipe for mashed potatoes is pretty basic and basically delicious. Okay, my mother did raise an eyebrow at the garlic, but you've got to have a little room to explore.

GARLIC MASHED POTATOES

Once a trend, now a classic.

{ S ERVES 8 . }

4   pounds thin-skinned, waxy potatoes
    Water to cover
1   tablespoon salt

5   cloves garlic, peeled
5   tablespoons butter
½   teaspoon or more black pepper
½   cup buttermilk (approximately)

 C lean the potatoes and place in a pot. Cover with water and add the salt and garlic cloves.

Bring to a boil and cook about 20 minutes until the potatoes are quite tender, but not falling apart. Drain the potatoes with the garlic. If you want to peel the potatoes, the skin will pull away very easily. Sometimes I like the added texture of the peel. Place the potatoes and garlic cloves, which will be very soft and mild in flavor now, in a large bowl and add the butter and pepper. Use a potato masher to smash 'em up, adding a little buttermilk to loosen them, but not so much as to make them sloppy. Taste for seasoning and adjust accordingly. Serve immediately or place in a casserole to reheat in the oven and get a crispy top.

POTATO AND PARSNIP PURÉE

You could also use turnips or salsify.

{ S ERVES 8. }

3   pounds thin-skinned, waxy potatoes
1   pound parsnips, peeled and cut in large chunks
1   tablespoon salt
½   teaspoon white pepper
½   cup butter
    Dash nutmeg
½   cup cream (approximately)

 C lean the potatoes and place in a pot with water 2 inches above the potatoes. Add the salt and pepper and bring to a boil. Add the parsnips and cook all until tender, about 15 minutes. Drain well and pull the skin from the potatoes. Place all in a food mill over a mixing bowl that holds the butter. Work the potatoes and parsnips through the food mill. Add the nutmeg to the potatoes and stir, incorporating the butter. Add the cream a little at a time until the desired consistency. Taste for seasoning and serve immediately.

SCALLOPED POTATOES

Be forewarned, this is a decadent and luscious dish.

{ SERVES 12. }

4   pounds thin skinned, waxy potatoes, such as Yukon Gold, Fingerling, or Yellow Finnish
1   large yellow onion
1½ cups cream
1   teaspoon salt
½   teaspoon white pepper
    Dash nutmeg
1½ cups grated cheese

Wash the potatoes and slice as thinly as possible with the skins on. Peel the onion and slice as thinly as possible. Layer the potatoes and onions in a casserole, sprinkling each layer with salt and pepper and a little cheese. Pour the cream over all and top with remaining cheese. Lightly sprinkle a little nutmeg on top. Cover with foil and bake at 350° until cooked through, testing with a knife, about 45 minutes. Remove the foil and brown the top. Serve hot.

This recipe makes a lot, but you will need a lot. I have never had any left over. In fact, I have discovered my guests in my kitchen after dinner, having at the crusty corners of the casserole with their fingers. This dish is rich and sinful and worth it.

COTTAGE FRIES

Growing up in the age of baked tater tots, homemade fries were a big treat for us. Even as a child, I could not get over how potato-ey they tasted compared to the frozen kind.

{ SERVES 6 TO 8. }

3   pounds potatoes, scrubbed clean and sliced in very thin circles (peel left on)
    Vegetable oil
    Salt and pepper to taste

Pour the oil in a deep cast iron skillet about two inches up. Heat the oil until very hot, but not smoking, about 325°. Fry the potatoes in batches, being careful not to overcrowd the pan. Drain the potatoes on paper bags placed over newspapers or a cardboard box. Salt and pepper and serve immediately.

POTATO PANCAKES

This is the way my mother always made potato pancakes, which we generally enjoyed for breakfast. We would pray for lots of leftover mashed potatoes on Saturday night so that we could wake up to these on Sunday.

{ SERVES 8. }

2   pounds mashed potatoes (about 1 quart), chilled
½   cup all-purpose flour
3   tablespoons vegetable oil (or butter, or, what the heck, bacon fat)

Form the mashed potatoes into eight 1/4-pound patties. Lightly dust with flour. Heat half the fat in a skillet and and cook half the pancakes, turning once, until browned. They'll stay together better if you place them in the hot fat and leave them alone for a few minutes, forming a crust, before you attempt to turn them.

We usually had these with bacon and eggs, but they're great with grilled chicken, salmon, or pork tenderloin for dinner.

ROASTED NEW POTATOES

An easy and truly tasty side dish. Vary the herbs to match your mood.

{ SERVES 6. }

2   pounds small new potatoes
¼   cup olive oil
½   teaspoon salt
    Black pepper to taste
1   tablespoon fresh minced herbs

Preheat the oven to 400°. Use smaller potatoes, if possible. Clean and quarter the potatoes. Be sure they are fairly dry. Place in a bowl and pour the olive oil over. Add salt and pepper and toss the potatoes to coat evenly. Place on a baking sheet and roast in the oven until cooked through and nicely browned, about 20 minutes. You may need to turn the potatoes once during cooking. Remove from the oven and toss with the fresh herbs. I like to choose just one herb. Rosemary is traditional, and delicious with strong game. Parsley or basil are both nice, mint is unexpected and refreshing. Your choice.

These are quite tasty served hot or at room temperature, but I can not abide them straight from the fridge.

RICE

Southerners have traditionally preferred a very fluffy white rice. In order to achieve this, rice is drained and well rinsed after it comes to a boil. This gets rid of most of the starch on the outside of the grains so that they don't stick together. Then you put the rice in a steamer and cook it very slowly.
This is a simpler and starchier version.

One popular type of rice is an aromatic long–grain rice from Louisiana called popcorn rice. When it is cooking, the entire house will actually smell just like there's popcorn cooking. It tastes as good as it smells, too.

{ SERVES 4. }

2   cups water
1   teaspoon salt
1   teaspoon butter
1   cup rice

Bring the water to a boil in a saucepan with the salt and butter. Stir in the rice and bring back to a boil. Stir once more, cover, and reduce the heat to very low. Cook for 15 minutes. Remove the lid and use a fork to fluff.

BAKED RICE

So simple and so good. This will work with everything.

{ SERVES 8. }

2   teaspoons butter
¼   onion, minced
1   cup rice
2   cups well-seasoned chicken stock
1   bay leaf

Preheat the oven to 325°. Melt the butter in a saucepan and add the onion, cooking just to wilt. Stir in the rice, coating all the kernels with the butter, until the rice looks slightly opalescent. Stir in the stock and the bay leaf and bring to a boil. Reduce heat, stir and cover. Bake for 20 minutes, discard the bay leaf, and serve hot.

SALSIFY

Salsify is one of those vegetables which you think you might recall from an obscure Jane Austin novel. Actually, salsify was grown quite extensively here in the mid–South until the last few decades. Also referred to as Oyster Plant, salsify is a great starchy tuber and may be baked and mashed like a potato.
This simple recipe adds a little herbal seasoning to a quick preparation.

Salsify is quite hairy and a bit frightening visually. Don't be alarmed. A paring knife will tame the beast.

{ SERVES 4. }

1   bunch salsify
    Juice of 1 lemon
3   tablespoons butter
1   tablespoon chopped parsley
1   teaspoon chopped chives

Wash and scrape the salsify. Place at once into cold water with the lemon juice. Bring a pot of salted water to a boil while cutting the salsify into 1-inch rounds. Cook the salsify in the boiling water until tender. Drain and return to the pan with the butter and additional salt and pepper to taste. Heat through, toss with the herbs, and serve.

Squash

Summer squash shares the same problem as most country and western music these days. There's too much of it and its basically bland and tasteless. However, just like Dwight Yoakim on a lonely night, there is yet some life and innocence in those tender little yellow gourds. Little is definitely the key word here. The larger a summer squash, the woodier, starchier, and less flavorful. We must also remember that summer squash really is pretty fragile. Leave it alone in a brown paper bag inside your fridge for more than a day or two, and you will open that bag to find a lifeless and shriveled shell of a vegetable. Spare yourself and the squash the degradation. Buy small, very fresh yellow crookneck squash and cook it up that night.

COUNTRY SQUASH

Just the thing with fried chicken in the summer.

{ SERVES 6. }

2	pounds yellow crookneck squash, cut in 1-inch thick circles
1	yellow onion, sliced
1	teaspoon salt
1	teaspoon black pepper
¼	teaspoon cayenne pepper
	Water
2	tablespoons bacon grease

Place the squash and onion with the salt and pepper in a heavy skillet and pour water about half way up. Bring to a boil. Stir, reduce the heat to medium, and cook until almost all of the water has evaporated. Add the bacon grease. Stir, reduce the heat to low, and continue to cook another 20 minutes, until the vegetables are cooked down and glossy.

STEAMED SUMMER SQUASH

Mama and Daddy have found a farmer at their market who brings in a variety of tiny little squash, crooknecks, zucchini, white patty pan, plus the golden round Sunburst. Mama combines these and lightly steams them on every possible night in the summer. They are truly beautiful, with a delicate, sweet flavor.
We, my baby included, nibble on any leftovers cold the next day.

{ SERVES 6. }

2   pounds small, very fresh yellow crookneck squash
     Water
½   teaspoon salt
     Pinch white pepper
2   tablespoons butter
     Juice of 1 lemon
1   tablespoon roughly chopped fresh dill

Clean the squash well and trim the ends. Pour 1 inch of water into a pan fitted with a steamer. Bring the water to a boil. Place the squash in the top part of the steamer and sprinkle with salt and white pepper. Place inside the steam bath and turn the heat to medium. Cover and steam for 7 minutes.

Remove the squash to a saucepan. Add the remaining ingredients and toss to melt the butter and coat the squash with all. Serve warm.

PATTY PAN SQUASH WITH CHEESE GRITS

These are so pretty and delicious, I'd serve them with a little tomato sauce underneath as a first course at a fancy seated dinner. They're also a great addition to roasts or barbecues.

{ SERVES 6. }

12	small patty pan squash
	Water
1	teaspoon salt
	Pinch white pepper
1	tablespoon olive oil (or butter)
½	yellow onion, diced
4	cloves garlic, minced
1	teaspoon tomato paste
3	cups water
1	cup grits
1	teaspoon salt
¼	teaspoon black pepper
1	teaspoon minced fresh sage
½	cup grated sharp Cheddar cheese

*B*ring the water to a boil with the salt. Add the squash and parboil about 2 minutes until just tender, depending on the size. Drain and cool. Scoop out about 1 tablespoon of squash from the body, using a spoon or melon baller.

Preheat the oven to 350°. Heat the olive oil in a saucepan and sauté the onion and garlic until translucent. Add the tomato paste and cook a couple of minutes, stirring. Pour in the water and bring to a boil. Stir in the grits and reduce the heat to medium. Cook for 20 minutes, stirring occasionally. Stir in the cheese and sage, and let cool slightly.

Spoon about 2 tablespoons of the grits into the hollow of the squash, mounding over the top. Place on a baking sheet and bake for 15 to 20 minutes, until heated through and slightly browned. These are nice on a picnic the following day.

SQUASH CASSEROLE

This is a great way to use up any larger or less than perfect squash with which you may be saddled.
The casserole holds well and is good the next day. Really nice for a summer buffet.

{ S E R V E S   8 . }

2   pounds yellow squash (older, larger squash may be used here)
1   yellow onion, diced large
    Water
1   tablespoon salt
1   cup breadcrumbs (plus more for topping)
3   eggs
1   cup cream
2   tablespoons minced fresh basil
1   teaspoon black pepper
    Dash cayenne pepper
½   cup plus ½ cup grated sharp Cheddar cheese

Preheat the oven to 350°. Clean the squash and cut in circles. Place in a pot along with the onion and cover with cold water. Add the salt and bring to a boil. Reduce the heat to medium and cook about 20 minutes until very tender. Drain well and place in a large mixing bowl. Add the breadcrumbs. Beat the eggs with the cream and mix into the squash. Stir in the fresh basil and ½ cup of grated cheese. Taste and add peppers and additional salt if needed. Pour into a baking dish and cover the top with additional breadcrumbs and the remaining ½ cup of grated cheese. Cover with aluminum foil. Bake at 350° for 30 minutes until the casserole is set.

Remove the foil and continue baking for 10 more minutes until browned on top.

BAKED SWEET POTATOES

Nature at its finest, merely heated up by man.

{ SERVES 8. }

4   sweet potatoes
¼   cup butter
     Salt and fresh ground black pepper to taste
     Dash ground cinnamon

Preheat the oven to 350°. Scrub the sweet potatoes clean and place right on the lower rack in the oven. Bake about 30 minutes until they are soft and squishy when squeezed. Cut the potatoes in half while they are still hot and stuff with butter. Sprinkle with salt, pepper, and cinnamon, and serve warm. I love these with lemon grilled chicken.

ROASTED SWEET POTATOES

So good I can eat a plate of them for dinner. A wonderful side for roast chicken in the fall.

{ SERVES 8. }

4   sweet potatoes
1   red onion
2   tablespoons olive oil
     Salt and fresh ground black pepper to taste

Preheat the oven to 400°. Scrub the potatoes clean and cut in quarters lengthwise. Cut these in halves. Likewise cut the peeled and cleaned red onion and place both on a baking sheet. Pour the oil over and toss with salt and pepper. Roast in the oven about 20 minutes until tender and browned. Use a spatula to turn if needed to avoid burning. Lower the temperature, if necessary, to cook and brown the potatoes without burning. Serve hot or at room temperature. These are nice for a picnic, too.

FRIED SWEET POTATOES

The only way my Daddy will eat them.

{ SERVES 8. }

4   sweet potatoes
    Vegetable oil
    Salt and pepper
    Pinch ground cinnamon, if desired

Scrub the sweet potatoes clean and slice in thin circles. Heat 1-inch of vegetable oil in a heavy pan until the oil is wavy and glassy, about 325°. Fry the sweet potatoes, in batches if necessary, until nicely browned all over. Drain on clean paper bags, sprinkle with salt and pepper, and serve hot. If you use the cinnamon, mix it in with the salt before sprinkling over the potatoes.

MASHED SWEET POTATOES

Smooth and satisfying. This is good living. Particular comforting when northern winds blow chilly and cold.

{ SERVES 6 TO 8. }

4   sweet potatoes
1   Granny Smith apple, cored and sliced (I like to leave the peel on)
¼   cup butter
    Juice and zest of 1 orange
    Salt and white pepper to taste
    Pinch allspice

Bake the sweet potatoes as directed on page 94. Place the apples on a baking sheet and bake at the same time as the potatoes. The apples should cook for about 20 minutes, the potatoes for 30, until they are soft.

Remove from the oven and peel away the skins from the potatoes while they are still hot. They should pull away very easily (Use a dish towel if your fingers are sensitive.) Place the sweet potatoes in a bowl and lightly mash, leaving some lumps. Add the apples along with the remaining ingredients and stir together. Place in a baking dish and return to the oven to heat through and brown the top for about 20 minutes.

This is the definitive side dish for grilled or roasted pork tenderloin, or pork chops, fried or baked.

Tomatoes

*T*omatoes are the vegetable that captures the very essence of summer. I hold them straight from the garden in my hands and feel their warmth and breathe their perfume intensified by the sun. Should I eat you up right now, or slice you and give you a dollop of homemade mayonnaise? Should I stuff you or broil you, bake or sauté you, or just cut you in wedges and drizzle you with olive oil? Perhaps I'll just set you up in my windowsill and look at you for awhile.

BROILED TOMATOES

A pretty, simple, and tasty vegetable. Really nice and fresh tasting with fish.

{ SERVES 6. }

2   ripe medium-sized tomatoes
    Salt
2   tablespoons dried breadcrumbs
2   tablespoons Parmesan cheese
1   tablespoon minced fresh basil
    Freshly ground black pepper to taste

*P*reheat the oven to broil. Wash the tomatoes and slice off the ends. Cut the tomato in 1½-inch slices (1 slice per serving) and place on a broiling pan. Sprinkle with salt and a little breadcrumbs and cheese. Top with basil and black pepper. Broil about 3 minutes, until the tomato is heated through and the topping is browned. Remove and serve immediately.

   Great with steaks or grilled chilled chicken or fish. Even winter tomatoes are nice like this.

FRIED GREEN TOMATOES

Yes, they are for real. In fact, they are really good. We used to fry them on cookouts when I was a nine-year-old camper in the Cumberland Mountains. Come to think of it, those were the best I've ever had. Now green tomatoes are a staple at Martha's.

{ SERVES 6 TO 8. }

4 green tomatoes
1 quart buttermilk
½ cup cornmeal
1 tablespoon all-purpose flour
1 teaspoon salt
1 teaspoon black pepper
¼ teaspoon cayenne pepper (or to taste)
¼ cup vegetable oil

Slice the tomatoes ½-inch thick. Place in a bowl and pour the buttermilk over the tomatoes, and allow them to soak while you prepare the breading.

Mix together the cornmeal, flour, salt, and black and cayenne pepper. Dredge the tomatoes in the coating on both sides and refrigerate for 30 minutes. This makes the coating stick.

Heat half the oil in a skillet and fry half of the tomatoes until browned on both sides, turning once, about 2 or 3 minutes per side. Drain on a clean paper bag and keep warm in a low oven.

Wipe out the skillet and heat the remaining oil. Fry the rest of the tomatoes, drain, and serve hot.

A classic breakfast with fried eggs and pork chops—great any time of the day.

TOMATOES STUFFED WITH HERBED RICE AND CHEESE

This is a perfect light supper with a green salad or some cucumbers. Makes a nice side dish for a summer buffet.
Feta cheese can be a tasty and less expensive alternative to the goat cheese.

{ SERVES 6. }

6	homegrown tomatoes
1	tablespoon olive oil
½	yellow onion, diced fine
1	cup rice
2	cups flavorful chicken or vegetable stock
1	bay leaf
1	teaspoon salt
1	teaspoon white pepper
	Juice and zest of 1 lemon
1	tablespoon minced fresh parsley
1	tablespoon minced fresh basil
1	tablespoon minced fresh mint
½	cup fresh goat cheese, crumbled (plus extra for topping)

Wash the tomatoes and slice off ½-inch at the tip end. Use a melon baller or small spoon to scoop out most of the pulp from the open tip end, being careful not to tear the sides. Reserve the pulp, discarding most of the seeds.

Heat the olive oil in a saucepan and stir in the onion. Cook until translucent. Stir in the rice and cook for a few minutes, until the kernels look pearly. Pour in the stock and stir, adding the bay leaf, salt and pepper. Bring to a boil. Stir, cover, and reduce the heat to low. Cover and cook for 15 minutes. Remove the lid and take off the heat. Discard the bay leaf and stir in the lemon juice and zest, herbs, and reserved tomato pulp. Allow to cool. Lightly stir in the crumbled cheese.

Preheat the oven to 350°. Stuff the tomato cavities full with the rice and top with a little additional cheese. Place the tomatoes core-side down on a baking sheet. Bake for about 20 minutes, until heated through and slightly browned on top.

Adding shrimp or crab meat to the rice makes a more substantial main course for a luncheon or light summer supper.

TOMATOES WITH CORN

A yummy, mid–summer vegetable stew. Serve it over rice or with white bean croquettes for a meal in itself.

{ SERVES 6. }

4   ripe tomatoes
2   ears corn
2   tablespoons olive oil
1   yellow onion, diced medium
½   bell pepper, diced medium (or 1 banana pepper, sliced in thin circles)
4   cloves garlic
2   teaspoons salt (or to taste)
    Fresh ground black pepper
½   cup red wine
    Juice of 1 lemon
1   tablespoon minced fresh basil
1   tablespoon minced fresh parsley
3   scallions, thinly sliced

Bring a large pot of water to a simmer. Fill a bowl with ice water. Rinse the tomatoes and cut out the core. Cut a slash in the tip end, and drop in the simmering water for about thirty seconds, until the skin pulls away easily. Use a slotted spoon to remove the tomatoes from the pot and drop into the ice water. Leave in the ice water until cool. Remove and drain in a colander. Pull away the skin and coarsely chop the tomatoes. Set aside in a bowl.

Shuck and clean the corn and cut the kernels from the cob. Set aside.

Heat the olive oil in a large skillet. Add the onion and cook until transparent. Add the pepper and garlic and cook, stirring occasionally, for 5 more minutes. Add the tomatoes along with the salt and pepper. Stir and cook for 5 minutes. Add the wine and lemon juice along with the corn. Stir, bring back to a simmer, and cook for 5 minutes. If the mixture is too runny, turn the heat to high and cook at a hard boil for a couple of minutes, being careful not to burn. Stir in the basil, parsley, and scallions, and serve immediately.

This could be a whole meal served over rice or pasta, or a great side dish for shrimp, fish, or chicken.

STEWED TOMATOES

Stewed tomatoes have been a conundrum to me. I love the idea, but for years and years every time I tried stewed tomatoes I almost spit them out. A case of too much sugar, and too little anything else. These stewed tomatoes finally work for me.

{ SERVES ABOUT 10. }

¼   cup butter
2   yellow onions, diced
8   ripe tomatoes, peeled and coarsely chopped
1   tablespoon salt
1   tablespoon firmly packed brown sugar
2   tablespoons cider vinegar
    Dash cayenne pepper

Heat the butter in a heavy saucepan, add the onions, and cook until translucent. Add all remaining ingredients, stir, and bring to a slow boil. Reduce the heat and cook uncovered, stirring frequently, for 30 minutes. The tomatoes should be thick and glossy.

BOILED TURNIPS BROWNED IN BUTTER

Simple and lovely. A nice alternative to boiled new potatoes.

{ SERVES 6 TO 8. }

4   medium turnips
2   tablespoons butter
    Salt and white pepper to taste
    Pinch nutmeg
1   teaspoon fresh parsley, minced

Peel the turnips and cut in large cubes. Place in a pot and cover with cold water. Add salt and bring to a boil. Reduce the heat to medium and cook about 10 minutes until tender but not mushy. Drain the turnips.

Heat the butter in a skillet and add the turnips, tossing to coat with the butter. Cook on medium about 7 minutes until browned, tossing occasionally. Sprinkle with salt, pepper, nutmeg, and parsley, and serve immediately.

These are nice with roast beef, turkey, or lamb. Flavorful and wholesome on a chilly evening.

{ *Chapter 6* }

FRITTERS AND
LITTLE FRIED THINGS

Frying is a maligned, misunderstood, and mis-practiced craft. The idea that all fried foods are greasy comes from not knowing how to fry. Many years ago the fat that we used to fry in contributed to a greasy feel and flavor because animal fat, or lard, with all of its impurities cannot heat to a very high temperature before it smokes and burns. Food that is fried in lard usually absorbs a lot of fat, is not very pleasant to feel in the mouth, and to most of us is not very tasty. Certainly it is not easily digestible. However, polyunsaturated vegetable oils available to us today can heat to a much higher temperature (325° to 350°) before smoking. Something that is fried at the proper temperature actually develops a crispy crust that doesn't allow the fat to seep through. A higher temperature cooks more quickly, intensifying the natural flavor of the food (you don't want to cook at too high a temperature, though, or the outside will burn, leaving the center uncooked). Furthermore, some vegetable oils, particularly peanut oil, which Asians have used to fry and sauté with for centuries, are almost completely neutral in flavor, adding nothing which would detract from the taste of whatever you are frying.

Not to suggest that a fritter a day keeps the doctor away. Common sense tells us fried foods will never be health foods, but good ones at least will always be soul food.

CORN FRITTERS

These tasty little morsels can be served as a bread or side, or make a great first course served with a spicy mayonnaise or just hot sauce.

{ SERVES 4 TO 6. }

2   cups corn kernels
1   tablespoon chopped parsley
1   tablespoon minced chives
1   teaspoon salt
½   teaspoon black pepper
¼   cup all-purpose flour
1   teaspoon baking powder
2   beaten eggs
     Vegetable oil

Stir all of the ingredients except the oil together in a mixing bowl. Let sit in the refrigerator for 1 hour. Pour 1 inch of vegetable oil in a heavy skillet and heat until you see waves cross the oil. Drop the fritters in the oil by spoonfuls and cook to brown on all sides. Drain on clean brown paper bags and sprinkle with salt before serving.

PARSNIP BALLS

These are great, a little pungent and spicy. Really good with roasted lamb or beef.

{ SERVES 6 TO 8. }

1   pound parsnips, peeled and cut in 1-inch pieces
2   teaspoons salt (plus
     additional, to taste)
½   teaspoons white pepper
     Dash grated nutmeg
½   cup all-purpose flour
2   eggs, beaten
     Vegetable oil

Place the parsnips in a pot and cover with water. Add the salt and bring to a boil. Cook about 10 minutes until the parsnips are tender. Drain, mash, and season with additional salt to taste, white pepper, and nutmeg. Add the flour and eggs, and chill about 1 hour until set. Pour 1 inch of vegetable oil in a heavy pot and heat to just under smoking, about 325°. Form the parsnip mixture into small balls and fry, turning to brown evenly.

Drain well and season with additional salt. I like to dip them in mustard.

LIMA BEAN CROQUETTES

I like to serve these with roast chicken and gravy.

{ SERVES 6. }

1½   pounds lima beans (frozen may be used)
1   teaspoon salt (plus
      additional, to taste)
4   eggs
½   teaspoon white pepper
½   teaspoon minced fresh sage
½   cup cream
3   cups fresh grated breadcrumbs
     Vegetable oil

Rinse the lima beans, if fresh. Bring a pot of water to boil with 1 teaspoon salt and boil the limas about 15 minutes until tender. Drain, place in a bowl, and mash. It shouldn't be completely smooth; you will still have lumps. Mix with 2 eggs, salt if need-ed, pepper, sage, and cream. Refrigerate for at least 1 hour.

Pour 1 inch of vegetable oil in a heavy pot or deep skillet and heat to just below smoking, about 325°. Beat the remaining 2 eggs. Shape the lima beans into small balls. Dip in the egg and then in the breadcrumbs. Fry until golden brown, turning, and drain on clean brown paper bags. Season with salt and serve.

WHITE BEAN CROQUETTES

Wonderful as a side for any meal. I like to serve them with tomato sauce and a green salad as a complete meal.

{ Serves 6 to 8. }

½   pound dry white beans
2   teaspoons salt (plus additional, to taste)
¼   teaspoon cayenne pepper
2   tablespoons butter
2   eggs
1   tablespoon chopped green onion
    Paprika
2   cups crushed cracker crumbs
    Vegetable oil

Place the beans in a pot with the salt and cover with water. Bring to a boil. Turn off the heat and let sit in the water for 1 hour. Drain, rinse, and place the beans back in the pot with 1 teaspoon salt, the cayenne, and water to cover. Bring to a boil and cook about 1 hour until very tender.

Beat 1 of the eggs. Drain the beans, mash slightly, and stir in the butter, 1 beaten egg, green onion, and paprika. Chill and form into balls.

Beat the remaining egg. Dip the balls in the egg, roll in the cracker crumbs, and chill again for 30 minutes.

Pour 1 inch of vegetable oil in a heavy pot or skillet. Heat to just under smoking, about 325°. Fry the croquettes until golden brown, turning to brown evenly. Drain on clean brown paper bags, sprinkle with salt, and serve with hot sauce or Tomato Sauce (see page 159).

RICE CROQUETTES

A perfect use for leftover rice. Great as an appetizer, or with any roasted meat.
Try breaking them open and ladling stew or hash over.

{ Serves 4 to 6. }

2　cups plain boiled rice

3　eggs

¼　onion, grated

1　teaspoon lemon juice

½　teaspoon salt

¼　teaspoon black pepper

1　tablespoon chopped parsley

2　tablespoons milk or cream

½　cup all-purpose flour

3　cups dry breadcrumbs

　　Vegetable oil

Mix the rice with 1 beaten egg, the onion, lemon juice, salt, pepper, parsley, and cream. Refrigerate for 30 minutes. Place the flour, 2 beaten eggs, and breadcrumbs in separate shallow dishes. Shape the rice mixture into balls. Roll lightly in the flour, dip in the egg, and roll in the breadcrumbs. Refrigerate for 30 more minutes.

　　Pour 1 inch of vegetable oil in a heavy pot or skillet. Heat to just under smoking, about 325°. Fry the croquettes until golden brown, turning to brown evenly. Drain on clean brown paper bags, season with salt, and serve.

SWEET POTATO CROQUETTES

A great sweet but savory accompaniment for turkey or pork.

{ SERVES 6. }

3	sweet potatoes
1	tablespoon butter
1	egg yolk
	Salt to taste
	Cayenne and white pepper to taste
	Dash ground cinnamon
½	cup chopped pecans
1	egg, beaten
2	cups dry breadcrumbs
	Vegetable oil

Preheat the oven to 350°. Rinse the sweet potatoes and bake for 30 minutes, until soft. Peel and mash while still hot, along with the butter and 1 egg yolk. Mix in the seasoning and nuts. Chill for 30 minutes. Form into balls, dip in the beaten egg, and roll in the breadcrumbs. Refrigerate while the oil is heating.

Pour 1 inch of vegetable oil in a heavy pot or skillet. Heat to just under smoking, about 325°. Fry the croquettes until golden brown, turning to brown evenly. Drain on clean brown paper bags, sprinkle with salt, and serve.

BREADING FOR GREEN TOMATOES, ONION RINGS, CATFISH, OYSTERS

This is an all-purpose breading mix for many things we make at the restaurant.
(Other methods appear individually throughout the book.) You can make a lot and just scoop out
what you think you'll need for whatever you're frying.

Cornmeal (1 part)

Flour (2 parts)

Salt

Pepper

Cayenne

In a shallow dish combine the ingredients. Store un-used dry breading in an airtight container for up to 1 month.

OKRA FRITTERS

A good way to use larger okra that you don't want to fry whole.

{ SERVES 4. }

2   cups all-purpose flour, sifted

1   teaspoon baking powder
    Salt and pepper to taste

2   eggs, beaten

1   cup butter milk

2   tablespoons cooking oil

2   cups cleaned, sliced okra
    Oil for deep frying

In a medium bowl sift together the flour, baking soda, salt and pepper. In a deep bowl combine the eggs, buttermilk, and oil. Add the dry ingredients, adding more buttermilk as needed to make a batter thick enough to stick to a spoon. Pour the oil into a deep skillet or pot, to a depth of 1 to 2 inches. Heat the oil to 330°.

Carefully spoon tablespoons of the the batter into the oil. Fry until golden brown, turning once or twice. Serve at once with Hot Pepper Jelly (see page 21).

HUSH PUPPIES

The mandatory accompaniment to any fish fry—any good one, that is.

{ SERVES 4 TO 6. }

2	cups white cornmeal
1	teaspoon baking powder
1	onion, finely chopped
2	stalks celery, finely chopped
1	cup buttermilk
¼	cup shortening, melted
½	teaspoon salt
¼	teaspoon black pepper
¼	teaspoon paprika
2	eggs
	Vegetable oil

Mix together everything but the oil. Refrigerate while the oil is heating. Pour 3 inches of vegetable oil in a deep skillet, or use a deep fat fryer. Drop the batter by tablespoonfuls into the hot oil and fry until golden brown. Drain on clean brown paper bags, sprinkle with salt, and serve hot with fried catfish, trout, shrimp, or oysters.

{ *Chapter 7* }

SEAFOOD

I've added quite a bit of seafood to our (new) new basics as our tastes and desire for healthier eating habits (i.e.eating more seafood) have changed, and the availability of fresh fish has increased. Unfortunately, that new "availability" is depleting our oceans' supply, and threatening some species very existence. It ain't always easy being human and doing the next right thing, is it? What we can try to do is be aware of that which species are threatened, and support responsible, sustainable fishing and aqua-culture. The Endangered Fish Alliance (endangeredfishalliance.org) is an excellent source of information.

I find that my cooking students are more intimidated by preparing seafood than anything else. Perhaps it's the cost, or the generally quick preparation. Perhaps it's that most of us who grew up in Nashville during my youth thought that fish-sticks were an exotic Friday treat. Regardless, learning to cook seafood is like learning anything. Familiarity and practice make it good. Be patient with yourself, and don't be afraid to make mistakes. It's only dinner. Besides, culinary disasters make for great family legends.

SCALLOPED OYSTERS

It took me the longest time to figure out why there have always been oysters in cookbooks and on bills of fare in land-locked Tennessee from the early eighteen hundreds on. Then I discovered that oysters were actually shipped live on ice and fed cornmeal throughout their journey.
One more good reason to traditionally eat oysters in the colder months.

Scalloped oysters are standard fare at many Thanksgiving dinners in the South. Rich and oh, so tasty, these are really quite simple to prepare.

{ SERVES 12. }

1	quart oysters
	Salt and black pepper to taste
	Cayenne pepper to taste
½	cup butter
	Juice of 1 lemon
1	quart soda cracker crumbs
1	scant cup cream

Preheat the oven to 400°. Place a layer of oysters in the bottom of a baking dish. Sprinkle with a little salt, pepper, and cayenne. Dot with butter, sprinkle with lemon juice, and layer cracker crumbs over. Arrange one or two more layers, ending in cracker crumbs. Pour the cream over just to moisten. Bake uncovered for 15 to 20 minutes and serve.

OYSTER STEW

This is an excellent winter meal. Simple and satisfying.

{ SERVES 6. }

4	slices bacon
1	onion, chopped
4	cloves garlic, minced
2	ribs celery, chopped
1	carrot, peeled and cut in ½-inch circles
1	teaspoon minced fresh thyme leaves

1   teaspoon minced fresh rosemary leaves

2   tablespoons all-purpose flour

4   cups milk

1   pint oysters with liquid

*C*ook the bacon and reserve. Pour the fat into a large saucepan and cook the onion for about 5 minutes, until wilted. Add the garlic, celery, carrot, thyme, and rosemary, and cook another 5 minutes. Stir in the flour and brown slightly. Stir in the milk and bring to a slight boil. Reduce to a simmer and cook for 15 minutes. Stir in the oysters and about half of the liquid, strained. Heat to just under boiling and cook until the oysters are slightly curled. Serve at once with rice or corn bread. Crumble bacon on top, if desired.

Be careful reheating this. The oysters can become chewy if boiled and the liquid may break. Best to serve immediately.

DEEP–FRIED OYSTERS

These make the best Po Boy Sandwich. But I usually just squeeze some lemon on them and pop them in my mouth.

{ S ERVES 4 TO 6 . }

24   large oysters

 1   teaspoon salt

¼   teaspoon black pepper

¼   teaspoon cayenne pepper

 2   eggs

 1   tablespoon water

 3   cups toasted breadcrumbs

     Oil for deep-frying

*P*ick through the oysters. Drain well and pat dry. Sprinkle with salt and peppers. Beat the eggs with the water in a shallow bowl. Place the bread crumbs on a plate. Roll each oyster in the breadcrumbs, then the egg, and again in the breadcrumbs. Refrigerate for 30 minutes. Heat the oil in a deep fat fryer to 325°. Fry the oysters for about 11/2 minutes, until golden brown. Drain on clean brown paper bags. Serve with Hush Puppies (see page 154), and Tartar Sauce (recipe follows).

TARTAR SAUCE

Yummy on French fries, too!

{ MAKES ABOUT 1 CUP. }

1   cup Mayonnaise (see page 29)
1   tablespoon sweet relish
    Juice of 1 lemon
    Dash cayenne pepper

Combine all of the ingredients in a medium bowl and mix well.

DEEP–FRIED FROGS' LEGS

Frogs' legs are a traditional food throughout the South. Commercially packed frogs' legs, large and meaty,
can be purchased frozen. And yes, they do taste quite a bit like chicken.

{ SERVES 2 TO 4. }

6   pair frogs' legs
    Boiling water
    Salt and pepper to taste
2   eggs, beaten
1   cup dry breadcrumbs
    Oil for deep-frying

Wash the frogs legs. Boil water and pour over. Let sit for 5 minutes. Drain and dry. Sprinkle with salt and pepper. Dip in the egg and dredge in the crumbs. Heat the oil in a deep fat fryer to 325°. Fry the frogs' legs for about 5 minutes. Drain on clean brown paper bags, sprinkle with salt, and serve with Tomato Sauce (recipe follows).

TOMATO SAUCE

Great with seafood, fried vegetables, meat loaf, and pasta. A great basic sauce to know.

{ Makes about 4 cups. }

2   tablespoons olive oil
1   large onion, finely chopped
1   red bell pepper, seeded and finely chopped
6   cloves garlic, minced
2   tablespoons tomato paste
1   28-ounce can tomatoes
½   cup red wine
2   teaspoons salt
1   teaspoon sugar
½   teaspoon dried oregano
½   teaspoon dried thyme
½   teaspoon dried basil
1   bay leaf

Heat the olive oil in a deep skillet or broad saucepan and add the onion. Cook on high for 5 minutes. Add the bell pepper and garlic and cook 5 more minutes, stirring occasionally to prevent burning the garlic, which gets very bitter if it burns. Stir in the tomato paste and cook a couple of minutes. Add the tomatoes, squeezing them with your hand to break them up and pouring in the juice from the tomatoes and the wine. Add the remaining ingredients, stir, and bring the mixture to a boil. Turn the heat to medium low and cook, stirring occasionally, for 1 hour.

Adjust the seasoning. Discard the bay leaf. This will be good for several days.

BOILED SHRIMP

Shrimp boiled in the shell will always give much more flavor than those that are first peeled.
Besides, getting a little messy is part of the fun with eating a plate of boiled shrimp.

I was taught the craft of boiling shrimp by one of my best friends, Steve Scalise, the executive chef at
The Corner Market in Nashville, who just happens to be from New Orleans. Like everything Steve cooks, it's more
of a method than a recipe. Improvisation is an important part of Steve's life in general.
And in life in general and boiling shrimp in particular, the seasonings can change. Just follow the time
and the how-to's. Steve's never failed me, and this won't fail you.

{ SERVES ABOUT 4 FOR A MAIN COURSE. }

3   pounds shrimp
1   gallon water
2   lemons, halved
2   green onions, rough chopped
3   sprigs parsley
1   celery stalk, roughly chopped
1   bay leaf
1   teaspoon salt
1   teaspoon cayenne pepper

*R*inse the shrimp and set aside, keeping them cool. Pour the water in a large pot with the the rest of the ingredients. Bring to rolling boil and cook for 5 minutes. Throw in the shrimp, bring back to a boil, and cook about 4 minutes. Don't overcook! You can see that the shrimp are cooked when the flesh pulls slightly away from the shell. Pull the pot off the heat and toss in a good sized bowl of ice. This will stop the cooking without rinsing away the flavors. If the ice melts very quickly, add some more. Let the shrimp steep in the liquid for 5 minutes, then drain and chill the shrimp in the fridge. Serve with Cocktail Sauce (recipe follows), lots of lemon, and plenty of paper towels.

COCKTAIL SAUCE

{ MAKES ABOUT 2½ CUPS. }

2　cups catsup
¼　cup prepared horseradish
　　Juice of 1 lemon
1　teaspoon hot sauce
2　cloves garlic, minced
¼　onion, grated

*M*ix together and serve with shrimp and oysters, boiled and fried.

DEEP-FRIED SHRIMP

Nashville is an eight-hour drive from the closest beach, the Redneck Riviera, or as most of the world knows it,
the Florida Panhandle. All jesting aside, these beaches are beautiful white sand, until recently quite pristine.
My parents became engaged down there, and as a family we spent a week there every year.
While we were vacationing, we always gorged ourselves on as much shrimp as we could possibly consume
and packed coolers with more to bring home. Deep-fried shrimp is a feast of celebration,
especially dear to us in this land-locked state.

{ SERVES 4 TO 6. }

　　Oil for deep-frying
3　pounds large shrimp
1　cup all-purpose flour
1　cup cornmeal
½　teaspoon garlic powder
½　teaspoon salt
½　teaspoon black pepper
1　tablespoon hot sauce

*H*eat the oil in a deep fryer to 325°. Peel and clean the shrimp, leaving the tail on. Mix the flour and meal with the seasonings on a plate. Pour the hot sauce on the shrimp and toss. Dredge the shrimp in the flour mixture and deep fry for about 3 minutes. Drain on clean brown paper bags, sprinkle with salt, and serve with lemon and Cocktail Sauce (recipe precedes) or Tartar Sauce (see page 158).

SHRIMP AND GRITS

This has become a classic at Martha's at the Plantation. I first had this in Savannah, then Charleston, and Sea Island. It's a Low Country kind of thing, and I'm happy whenever I'm in Low Country!

Shrimp and Grits is great for brunch—hearty enough for the "beefiest" male, but even the "low-carb" ladies ask for seconds.

The secret is the gravy!

{ SERVES 6 TO 8. }

FOR THE GRAVY:

1 quart milk
½ red onion, diced
2 teaspoons fresh minced garlic
3 ounces country ham, finely chopped
1 teaspoon seafood base
⅓ cup all-purpose flour
1 28-ounce can chopped tomatoes
½ teaspoon black pepper

In a saucepan warm the milk on top of the stove. Do not boil.

Melt the butter in a saucepan, add the onion, and cook 5 minutes. Add the country ham and garlic and cook 5 minutes more.

Stir in the seafood base, then the flour to make a roux. Whisk in the milk and bring to a simmer. Add the tomatoes and pepper. Bring back to a simmer and cook for 30 minutes.

FOR THE SHRIMP:

3 pounds large shrimp, peeled and deveined
   Salt and pepper to taste
5 tablespoons olive oil

Season the shrimp with salt and pepper and sear in batches. Heat 1 tablespoon of olive in a large skillet. Add 1 pound of shrimp. Cook for 2 minutes per side. Remove from the pan and keep warm while you cook the other 2 batches.

FOR THE GRITS:

2	cups water
2	cups half and half
1	teaspoon salt
½	teaspoon white pepper
2¼	cups grits
1½	cups buttermilk
5	eggs, beaten
2	cups grated Parmesan cheese

*B*ring the water and half and half to a boil with the salt and pepper. Whisk in the grits and cook to thicken, about 5 minutes.

Meanwhile, preheat the oven to 325°.

Beat the buttermilk with the eggs. Stir into the thickened grits, then stir in the Parmesan. Pour into a Pyrex baking dish. Bake about 30 minutes, until puffed and browned into delightful yumminess.

To serve, on each plate place a liberal heap of grits, then gravy, then seared shrimp. Garnish with chopped flat leaf parsley.

LOW COUNTRY BOIL

This is a great meal for a crowd—an event unto itself! I like to prepare it outside on propane-heated burners. We line a picnic table with butcher paper and turn out the drained "assemblage" directly onto that. A messy feast ensues!

{ SERVES 10 TO 15. }

3	boxes Zatarain's shrimp boil
3	pounds red new potatoes
3	pounds kielbasa
6	whole heads garlic, cut in half width-wise
5	pounds large shrimp

*I*n a large kettle place the shrimp boil seasonings, potatoes, kielbasa, and garlic, and cover generously with water. Bring to a boil on the stove or outdoor cooker. When the potatoes are tender, add the shrimp. Cook for about 3 minutes, until the shrimp are pink in color. Drain and serve.

SHRIMP CREOLE

A tried and true favorite. Quick and delicious.

{ SERVES 6 TO 8. }

3 tablespoon olive oil

1 medium onion, chopped

3 stalks celery, chopped

1 green bell pepper, thinly sliced

2 cloves garlic, chopped

1 pinch thyme leaves, crumbled

1 dash cayenne pepper

2 bay leaves

1 14.5-ounce can tomatoes, undrained

1 tablespoon tomato paste

3 pounds medium shrimp, peeled

Hot, cooked rice

6 to 8 green onions, chopped

In a heavy skillet heat the oil and sauté the onions, celery, bell pepper, garlic, thyme, cayenne pepper, and bay leaves for a few minutes, or until the vegetables are just tender.

Add the tomatoes and tomato paste; simmer 15 minutes. Add peeled the raw shrimp; simmer 10 minutes. Serve over steamed rice. Garnish with chopped green onions.

BBQ SHRIMP

Steve Scalise, my Cajun/Sicilian culinary mentor from Downtown New Orleans, kept his recipe for BBQ folded up in his back pocket. I believe the recipe was in his billfold, but he was always so stealthy in its retrieval that I can't be certain.

Now I know that Steve had probably memorized the ingredients and method of this simple recipe. I believe that bringing the yellowed parchment to light was a bit of ritual reserved for only the most sacred incantations and concoctions. With all of the recipes that Steve taught me to cook, he never shared the recipe for BBQ shrimp. This is an approximation, but I'm pretty good at recognizance work.

{ SERVES ABOUT 10 TO 12. }

1   pound (4 sticks) butter
½   cup catsup
¼   cup Louisiana Hot Sauce
2   teaspoons Italian seasoning
1½ tablespoons minced fresh garlic
2   tablespoons thin sliced green onions
2   tablespoons roughly chopped Italian parsley
    Juice of 2 lemons shrimp
3   dozen extra large shrimp, in the shell

In a heavy skillet melt the butter and add the remaining ingredients except the shrimp.

Stir and simmer for 10 minutes for the flavors to marry. Add the shrimp and turn the heat up to medium high. Cook for 3 to 5 minutes, until just cooked through (the shrimp will begin to pull away from the shell). Turn off the heat and let the shrimp sit in the sauce for 10 or so minutes.

Serve warm with lots of sauce and good French bread to sop up any leftovers. It's a good idea to spread newspapers out over your serving table.

CRAWFISH CAKES

*These are always on the menu at Martha's. They're an inexpensive alternative to crab cakes,
and people love them! We serve baby-sized cakes at parties, too.
Frozen crawfish tails are available (pre-cooked) in most grocery stores.*

{ MAKES 8 CRAWFISH CAKES, 3 TO 4 SERVINGS }

4   ounces (1 stick) butter
½   red onion, diced
2   sticks celery, diced
1   poblano pepper, diced
1   teaspoon chopped fresh garlic
½   teaspoon Italian seasoning
1   pound frozen crawfish tails, thawed
2   eggs
1   cup dry bread crumbs
    Grated zest and juice of 1 lemon
1   teaspoon salt
    Pinch black pepper
    Pinch cayenne pepper
1   teaspoon Louisiana Hot Sauce
2   teaspoons chopped flat leaf parsley

In a large sauté pan heat the butter. Add the onion and cook for 3 minutes. Add the poblano pepper, celery, garlic, and Italian seasoning, and cook 3 minutes more. Set aside.

Place the crawfish tails in the bowl of a food processor fitted with a steel blade and pulse until the crawfish is very finely minced.

Place the sautéed vegetables and crawfish in a large mixing bowl along with the remaining ingredients. Mix together thoroughly. Make a small "tester" cake and fry in a small amount of vegetable. Taste and adjust the seasonings. Form the mixture into cakes and fry in vegetable oil. Drain and serve with Remoulade (recipe follows) and Black-Eyed Pea Salsa (see page 40).

REMOULADE

This is not a classic remoulade, but my quick, throw-together version. It's good on almost anything!

{ MAKES 3 CUPS. }

1   cup mayonnaise
1   cup sour cream
1   cup grainy mustard

*I*n a medium bowl combine all of the ingredients and mix well.

SALMON BALLS

These probably became popular in the mid-South because you could make them with canned salmon,
the only kind available until very recently. You could, of course, cook fresh salmon,
but a quality canned brand works fine for these.

{ SERVES 4. }

1   cup flaked salmon
2   medium potatoes
½   teaspoon salt
¼   teaspoon black pepper
1   teaspoon lemon juice
1   tablespoon fresh chopped parsley
2   teaspoons sliced green onions
1   egg
     Oil for deep-frying

*P*ick through the salmon and refrigerate until ready to use. Cook the cleaned potatoes with skins on in salted water as for mashed potatoes until easily pierced with a fork. Peel and mash. Beat 1 cup of the mashed potatoes with the salmon and other ingredients except the oil. Refrigerate for 30 minutes.

   While the salmon mixture is cooling, heat the oil in a deep fat fryer to 325°. Form the mixture into balls and fry until golden brown. Drain on clean brown paper bags, sprinkle with salt, and serve with lemon.

FRIED BROOK TROUT

Beautiful trout grace the streams throughout the mid–South. This makes a very tasty breakfast for hungry fishermen just home with their catch. Thankfully, fresh trout is available at just about every seafood counter, so you can have this for breakfast, lunch, or dinner, fishermen friends or no.

{ Serves 4. }

4 fresh brook trout, cleaned
   Salt and pepper to taste
   Dash paprika
½ cup all-purpose flour
1 egg
1 cup dry breadcrumbs
   Vegetable oil

Rinse the fish and pat dry. Sprinkle with the salt, pepper, and paprika. Heat ½ inch of vegetable oil in a heavy skillet. Lightly run the fish through the flour, dip in the egg, and then dredge in the crumbs. Place cut-side down in the hot oil and fry for 11⁄2 minutes. Turn and fry for 1½ minutes more. Drain well and serve with lots of lemon.

FRIED CATFISH

The stuff that dreams are made of. Catfish is so creamy and light. You can prepare it a number of perhaps more healthful ways, but this is by far its most common form and a true taste sensation and flavor delight.

{ Serves 6. }

6 nice-sized catfish fillets
1½ cups buttermilk
½ cup all-purpose flour
½ cup cornmeal
   Salt and pepper to taste
   Vegetable oil
2 lemons, cut in wedges

Rinse the catfish. Pour the buttermilk in a shallow bowl and set the fish in this in the refrigerator for 1 hour. Mix the flour and meal with the salt and pepper. Pour 1⁄2 inch of oil in a heavy skillet and heat to just under smoking. Lift the fish from the milk and dredge in the flour mixture. Place inside-side down in the oil and fry for about 4 minutes per side. Drain and serve with lemon.

TROUT WITH LEMON CAPER SAUCE

Frequently called trout "meuniere" (which is French for fisherman's wife), this simplest of preparations is so good for really fresh fish.

{ SERVES 6. }

6 large trout fillets
1½ cups all-purpose flour
1½ teaspoons salt
½ teaspoon pepper
6 tablespoons butter
2 tablespoons minced parsley
1 tablespoon lemon juice
1 teaspoon capers

*R*inse the trout filets and pat dry. In a shallow dish mix the salt and pepper with the flour and dredge the fillets in the flour mixture.

In a large frying pan melt the butter and sauté the fillets for 5 minutes. Turn the fish and sauté the other side for about 4 minutes.

Put the trout on a warm serving dish and sprinkle with a little more salt and pepper.

Add the lemon juice and the parsley to the butter remaining in the pan and heat until foamy. Pour over the trout and serve.

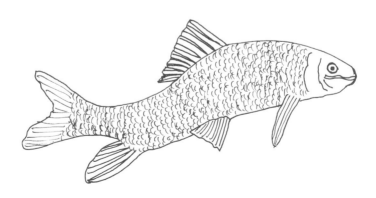

BAKED GROUPER WITH TOMATOES AND CITRUS

Quick, easy, healthy, and delicious.

{ SERVES 4. }

4   6-ounce grouper fillets
3   tablespoons olive oil
    Salt and pepper to taste
2   fresh tomatoes, chopped
1   cup grapefruit sections
2   teaspoons fresh minced garlic
1   teaspoon fresh thyme leaves
3   scallions slice thinly

Preheat the oven to 450°. Rinse the fillets and pat dry. Place on a baking sheet with sides and top with the remaining ingredients. Bake for 5 to 10 minutes, until cooked through but still moist. Serve over rice or buttered pasta.

GRILLED TUNA

This is the simplest way I know to grill tuna. Just last night I prepared this and placed the tuna over a salad of baby spinach, grape tomatoes, and fresh mango. The dressing (Burnt Sugar Vinaigrette, page 66), also became the sauce for the fish.

{ SERVES 4 FOR LUNCH OR LIGHT SUPPER. }

4   4-ounce tuna medallions
4   tablespoons Mayonnaise (see page 29)

Rinse the tuna and pat dry. Place in a Pyrex dish, and dollop a tablespoon of mayonnaise over each. Spread evenly all over the surface. Let sit, covered, in the refrigerator for at least 30 minutes or overnight.
    Prepare a grill to medium.
    Cook the tuna on the grill for 5 minutes each side for medium.

{ Chapter 8 }

POULTRY

The South is not alone in its love affair with poultry. Particularly in these low-fat days, I feel that poultry is frequently lauded as the perfect protein. I myself am re-romanced by free range chicken, organic, that is, chicken as our grandparents knew it on the farm. Chicken with a little color to its meat, not bleached pure white by chemicals, hormones, and synthetic feed. Chicken that has a taste of poultry, not cardboard. Obviously, free range chicken is more expensive, prohibiting most of us from eating it three or four nights a week. But maybe if more and more of us sample this higher quality chicken and are introduced to what chicken or poultry can really taste like, maybe then more of us will demand it and more suppliers will supply it. That, my friends, is how the price comes down. Democracy and a free market in action. Glory be.

FRIED CHICKEN

Where would we be without fried chicken? What would we have eaten at all of those picnics and Sunday dinners?
Would our accents be different? Would we walk with a quicker gate? Luckily these are frightening questions that
we need not ponder, for there has always been and will always be fried chicken in the South.

After contemplating the many methods of frying chicken with all of their nuances, advantages, and disadvantages,
I settled on one method which, quite frankly, makes a damn good fried chicken.

{ ABOUT 8 SERVINGS. }

4	pounds cut-up chicken pieces, your choice
1½	cups buttermilk
1	cup self-rising flour
1	teaspoon salt
1	teaspoon black pepper
¼	teaspoon cayenne pepper
½	teaspoon garlic powder
1	teaspoon paprika
1	egg
	Vegetable oil

Rinse the chicken pieces and soak in 1 cup buttermilk in the refrigerator for at least
2 hours or overnight.
Stir together the flour and seasonings and place on a plate. Beat the egg together with
the remaining buttermilk. Heat oil about 1 inch deep in a skillet.
Remove the chicken from the buttermilk and dredge in the flour. Dip in the egg mixture,
then dredge again in the flour. Fry until cooked through, about 15 to 20 minutes. Drain
on clean brown paper bags and season with salt.

FRIED LIVERS AND GIZZARDS

People get really funny about just what innards they will and will not eat. I myself am a born liver lover,
but I would not deign to nibble on a gizzard. I've been told it goes both ways. Some gizzard people
hate the texture of livers. Luckily, especially if both camps dwell in your home, they both are cooked
the same way for about the same amount of time.

Prepare just as you would for fried chicken, but cut the cooking time down to 5 to 7
minutes. Serve with gravy.

CHICKEN GRAVY

Some people seem frightened of gravy, but, I promise you, there is no great mystery here.
If you do get some little lumps, just pour it through a strainer.

$\mathcal{P}$our all but 3 tablespoons of the fat from the frying pan, leaving the crumbs left from the chicken. Add 3 tablespoons of all-purpose flour, and cook, stirring constantly, until lightly browned, but not burnt, or it will be hopelessly bitter. Slowly add 2½ cups of good chicken stock. Stir and cook slowly about 20 minutes until the gravy is browned and thickened. Season with salt and pepper, and serve separately from the chicken.

A lot of people use milk instead of water.

GRILLED CHICKEN LIVERS

I adore chicken livers, one of many culinary passions I shared with my Daddy.
Daddy would have narrowed his eyes as he watched from the sofa while I prepared these little kabobs—a little
high falutin' for him. But he would have eaten them, and looked around for more.

{ About 3 to 4 servings. }

1 pound chicken livers
2 tablespoons olive oil
1 teaspoon minced fresh garlic
½ teaspoon salt
   Black pepper to taste
8 fresh rosemary stalks

Prepare a grill to medium.

Cut the livers in havles and trim off any icky stuff. In a shallow dish combine the olive oil, garlic, salt, and pepper, and marinate the livers. Pull most of the leaves from the rosemary stalks. Skewer the livers on the stalks and grill about 5 minutes, turning midway through.

CHICKEN AND DUMPLINGS

This smells and tastes like somebody loves you.

{ SERVES 8. }

3 pounds chicken pieces
1 onion, chopped
3 stalks celery, chopped
2 carrots, peeled and chopped
1 bell pepper, chopped
3 cloves garlic, minced
2 bay leaves
1 teaspoon dried thyme leaves
4 sprigs parsley
2 teaspoons salt
½ teaspoon black pepper
   Dash cayenne pepper

Rinse the chicken and place in a Dutch oven with the remaining ingredients. Cover with cold water and bring to a slight boil. Reduce the heat to low, cover, and simmer until tender, about 1 hour or more. Remove the chicken pieces and, when cool enough to handle, skin and bone them, leaving the meat in large chunks. Leave the meat out of the pot as you prepare the dumplings (recipe follows).

BISCUIT DUMPLINGS

{ SERVES 8. }

1 cup all-purpose flour
2 teaspoons baking powder
½ teaspoon salt
½ cup milk

Skim as much fat as possible from the top of the broth. Heat the broth to a slow steady boil. Mix together the flour, baking powder, and salt. Stir in the milk and beat until stiff. Drop by spoonfuls into the boiling broth. Cover and cook for 10 minutes Add the meat back in and cook 5 more minutes. The dumplings should be puffed and the meat warmed through. Serve hot.

CREAMED CHICKEN

Yummy, smooth and as comforting as a favorite blanket.

{ SERVES 6. }

4   chicken breasts
1   onion, halved
1   stalk celery
2   teaspoons salt
½   teaspoon white pepper
1   bay leaf

¼   cup butter
½   onion, minced
¼   cup all-purpose flour
2   cups milk
¼   teaspoon salt
    White pepper to taste
    Dash nutmeg

Rinse the breasts and place in a pot. Cover with cold water, add 1 onion, the celery, and the seasonings, and bring to a boil. Reduce the heat to a simmer and cook about 15 minutes until tender. Remove the chicken and let cool. Strain the broth and return to the stove on low heat. Let the broth reduce on low while you finish preparing the chicken.

Melt the butter in a saucepan. Add the onion and cook until wilted. Stir in the flour. Cook about 5 minutes, stirring constantly. Slowly add the milk, stirring or whisking out any lumps. If you still have lumps, don't fret. You can strain the sauce later. Cook the sauce for 20 minutes. The sauce should not have any flour taste left to it. Add the chicken and thin the sauce out some with about ½ cup of the reduced broth. Taste and season accordingly (your broth could be pretty salty by now). Let the chicken heat through and serve over steamed rice, popovers, or cornmeal waffles.

CHICKEN BAKED IN RICE

This makes for a wonderfully robust dinner. I like to serve chicken and rice with something a little sweet,
like fried apples, and maybe a simple spinach salad.

{ SERVES 4. }

4   skin-on bone-in chicken breasts
¼   cup olive oil or butter
½   onion, chopped
3   cloves garlic, minced
3   ribs celery, chopped
2   cups rice
1   pint mushrooms, cut in quarters
4   cups good chicken broth
    Juice of 1 lemon
1   teaspoon dried thyme
1   bay leaf
2   teaspoons salt
½   teaspoon black pepper

*P*reheat the oven to 375°. Rinse the chicken breasts and pat dry. Season with salt and pepper. Heat the oil or butter in a heavy ovenproof saucepan wide enough to hold the breasts. Place the breasts skin-side down in the pan and sprinkle the onion around the breasts. When the onion begins to soften, add the garlic and celery. Turn the chicken to brown both sides. When both sides are lightly browned and the vegetables are wilted, stir in the rice to coat with fat. Stir in the mushrooms, stock, lemon juice, and the seasonings, and bring to a light boil. Stir and cover. Bake for 20 minutes until the rice is done and all of the stock is absorbed.

This makes a lot of rice, but it is so delicious, you'll be happy to have some left over, if indeed you do.

CHICKEN ARTICHOKE CASSEROLE

Our most requested one–dish meal for buffets and home entertaining.

{ SERVES 6 TO 8. }

4   chicken breasts
    Salt and pepper to taste
¼   teaspoon garlic powder
½   teaspoon Italian seasoning
¼   cup (½ stick) butter
½   yellow onion, chopped
2   stalks celery chopped
2   carrots, chopped
1   pint mushrooms, quartered
4   tablespoons all-purpose flour
2   cups chicken stock
1   cup cooked wild rice
1   cup cooked long-grain white rice
1   small can artichoke heart quarters, drained
½   cup plus ½ cup fresh grated Parmesan cheese
4   tablespoons dried or fresh breadcrumbs
2   tablespoons fresh chopped parsley

Preheat the oven to 400°. Rinse the chicken breasts and pat dry. Place on a baking sheet and sprinkle with salt, pepper, garlic powder, and Italian seasoning. Bake for 10 to 15 minutes, until cooked through, but still moist. Let cool and tear apart in bite size pieces.

Melt the butter in a large saucepan and add the onion. Cook for 2 minutes. Add the celery, carrot, and mushrooms. Stir and cook 5 minutes. Add the flour, stir, and cook 1 or 2 minutes. Add the stock and bring to a simmer. Stir and cook 5 minutes.

Pour into a mixing bowl, along with the chicken, rices, artichoke hearts, and half of the Parmesan. Mix well, but don't over mix. Turn out into the prepared casserole dish. Sprinkle with the breadcrumbs, remaining Parmesan, and parsley. Bake for 20 minutes. Serve warm.

CHICKEN POT PIE

This is one of the first main courses that I really started to play with as a budding young cook.
You can put any combination of complementary vegetables in here. Sometimes I use sweet potato or winter squash
for a little sweetness. Try lima beans or corn. Mama makes a great chicken pie with pork sausage, too.
The possibilities are endless.
You can also use any form of cooked chicken you may have, but this method supplies you with a rich broth,
as well. You should have enough left over to make some soup.

{ S E R V E S 6 . }

1	whole chicken
	Cold water to cover
2	onions
3	ribs celery
2	bay leaves
4	sprigs fresh thyme (or 1 teaspoon dried)
4	or 5 sprigs parsley
1	tablespoon salt
1	teaspoon white pepper
½	teaspoon cayenne pepper

¼	cup butter
1	onion, chopped
2	ribs celery, chopped
2	carrots, peeled and cut in ½-inch pieces
2	parsnips, peeled and cut in ½-inch pieces
½	pound mushrooms, cut in quarters
¼	cup frozen small peas
¼	cup all-purpose flour
2	cups chicken broth (or more)
1	teaspoon fresh thyme leaves
1	tablespoon chopped parsley
1	scallion, cut in thin circles

*R*inse the chicken well and remove the giblets. You may cook the neck with the chicken, but not the other stuff. Place the chicken in a large pot and cover with cold water. Add the 2 onions, 3 ribs of celery, bay leaves, sprigs of fresh thyme, sprigs of parsley, salt, pepper, and cayenne, and bring to a boil. Skim off any scum and turn the pot down to a simmer. Simmer for about 40 minutes.

Remove the chicken and let cool. Strain the broth and, if you like, you can simmer the broth, reducing it and getting a more concentrated flavor. Reduce, if you wish, for about 30 minutes.

Meanwhile, remove the skin from the chicken and pull the meat from the bones. Cool until ready to use.

Melt the butter in a large skillet and sauté the chopped onion until wilted. Add the chopped celery, carrots, parsnips, mushrooms, and peas, and cook for about 10 minutes. Reduce the heat, stir in the flour, and cook, stirring constantly, for about 5 minutes, letting the flour brown slightly. Slowly pour in the broth, stirring constantly. The sauce will thicken. Let the thickened sauce cook slowly for about 10 minutes, adding more stock if the sauce is too thick. . Stir in the chicken and fresh herbs and adjust the seasoning. Remove from the heat and pour all into a baking dish.

Preheat the oven to 400°. Make up one recipe of Buttermilk Biscuit dough (see page 221). Roll out ½-inch thickness and cut to cover the top of the baking dish. Place the cut out dough over the filling. Cut slits in the dough and brush with melted butter. Bake for about 10 to 15 minutes until the pastry is puffed and brown.

CHICKEN CROQUETTES

Mother is the great chicken croquette maker in our family. We tend to have these frequently for birthday parties, but they are one thing the entire extended family really loves.

I've also made smaller croquettes for large buffets.
Nice because they're tasty at room temperature as well as hot.

{ SERVES 6. }

Cook and pull chicken as you did for creamed chicken (see page 175) and prepare the white sauce, leaving out the extra broth. Cut the chicken meat into small pieces and place the chicken in a bowl along with the juice of 1 lemon, half of an onion, finely minced, and 1 rib of celery, finely minced. Pour just enough white sauce in to bind the chicken; it should not be too saucy. Taste for seasoning. You may need additional salt and pepper. Let the mixture cool for an hour or so to firm up. Grate 4 cups of fresh breadcrumbs and beat 2 eggs. Form the chicken into balls a little larger than golf balls. Roll in the breadcrumbs, dip in the egg, and then roll in the breadcrumbs again, pressing the crumbs in.

Refrigerate the croquettes while you heat vegetable oil in a deep fat fryer. When the oil has reached 325°, fry the croquettes a few at a time, draining them on box tops lined with clean brown paper bags. Makes about 18 small croquettes, to serve six. Serve with Giblet Gravy (see page 188).

CHICKEN PIQUANT FOR BARBECUE

This has a subtle, tangy flavor that I love. You can bake it fully in the oven if a grill isn't convenient,
but you won't get the same flavor.

{ SERVES 6. }

½   onion, grated

3   cloves garlic, minced

1   teaspoon salt

¼   cup chopped parsley

1   teaspoon dry mustard

¼   teaspoon black pepper

1   teaspoon Worcestershire sauce

1   tablespoon Louisiana-style hot sauce

6   tablespoons olive oil

6   large pieces bone-in skin-on chicken, leg or breast quarters

Combine all of the ingredients except the chicken and place in a baking dish. Rinse the chicken and let marinate in the baking dish for at least 1 and up to 12 hours. The chicken will get spicier the longer it marinates.

Preheat the oven to 375°. Cover the chicken in the marinade with aluminum foil and bake for 30 minutes. Remove the chicken from the marinade and broil on a medium hot grill until cooked through with a crispy skin.

Serve with Potato Salad (see page 67), Cole Slaw (see page 68), and a couple of other things, too.

RUB FOR GRILLED CHICKEN

I like to keep this seasoning rub on hand at home. It's an easy way to flavor chicken (or pork or beef!) in a hurry.

{ MAKES ABOUT ¼ CUP. }

- 4   tablespoons cumin
- 1   tablespoon salt
- ½   teaspoon cayenne pepper
- ½   teaspoon cinnamon
- ½   teaspoon granulated garlic
-     Olive oil

*I*n a small bowl combine the cumin, salt, cayenne, cinnamon, and garlic, and mix well.

CHIPOTLE BBQ SAUCE

Wonderful with grilled chicken… French fries, too!

{ MAKES ABOUT 3 CUPS. }

- 2   cups ketchup
- ½   cup soy sauce
- ½   cup honey
- ¼   cup hot sauce
- ¼   cup Dijon mustard
- 1   chipotle pepper plus 1 tablespoon of sauce from can
- 1   teaspoon black pepper
- 1   tablespoon minced fresh garlic

*I*n a medium saucepan combine all of the ingredients and mix well. Heat to a simmer and cook for 15 minutes. Keeps covered in the refrigerator for up to 1 month.

MARINATED GRILLED CHICKEN

This is how we prepare chicken for Plantation Salad (see page 66).

{ S E R V E S 6 . }

¼   cup olive oil
    Juice and zest of 2 lemons
2   teaspoons minced fresh garlic
1   tablespoon chopped flat leaf parsley
1   tablespoon chopped green onions
1   teaspoon salt
½   teaspoon black pepper

6   boneless, skinless chicken breasts

In a small bowl combine the olive oil, lemon zest and juice, garlic, parsley, onions, salt, and pepper. Mix together well. In a Pyrex baking dish arrange the chicken breasts and pour the marinade over them. Marinate for at least an 30 minutes, or overnight if possible.

    Grill for 5 minutes per side. Top with Brie for the Plantation Salad, or serve with Mint and Parsley Pesto (see page 204).

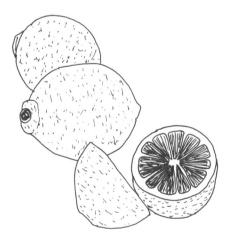

ROAST CHICKEN

Hard to resist when it's really done well. Leftovers make the best sandwiches.

{ SERVES 2 TO 4. }

1   roasting chicken
1   onion, quartered
1   bay leaf
3   cloves garlic, mashed
2   tablespoons butter, somewhat softened
    Juice of 1 lemon
1   teaspoon salt
¼   teaspoon black pepper
¼   teaspoon cayenne pepper
1   teaspoon fresh thyme leaves

Preheat the oven to 400°. Remove the giblets and rinse the chicken inside and out. Pat dry. Sprinkle some salt and pepper inside the body and stuff in the onion and bay leaf. Truss the chicken very simply by tying the legs together at the bottom joint and tying the wings up close to the body. There are a zillion ways to do this. Do what works for you. The idea behind trussing is not to make a perfect football shape for beauty's sake, but to get all of the parts held up close to the body in order to insure even cooking time. Trussing should not be a stressful experience.

Mash the garlic through a press or in a mortar and pestle with the salt sprinkled over. Mix with the butter, lemon, and the rest of the seasonings. Rub this paste all over the chicken, particularly getting up under the skin and rubbing on the meat itself. Place the chicken breast-side down on a rack inside a roasting pan and place in the oven at 400°. After 10 minutes, turn the oven down to 350°. Jiggle the chicken a bit to keep the breasts from sticking to the rack. Roast for 30 minutes.

Turn the chicken over to brown the breasts. Roast for at least 10 more minutes breast-side up, until a thermometer inserted in the thick of the thigh joint registers at least 160°. Let the chicken rest for 10 minutes before carving.

You may use the drippings from the bottom of the pan to make a gravy. Pour them into a saucepan and heat. Stir in about 3 tablespoons of flour and cook until the flour browns slightly. Stir in 2 cups of good chicken stock, stirring constantly. Bring to a boil and turn down to a simmer. Season with salt and lots of pepper and let cook for 20 minutes. Serve in a gravy boat.

HOT CHICKEN

Hot chicken is a bit of a phenomenon in Nashville, with Prince's Hot Chicken being the best known spot to find it.
Prince's chicken is not for the faint at heart. I understand that Prince is not eager to give up his recipe,
but I have concocted a method for more delicate palates (adjust as you wish.)

{ SERVES 6. }

2   cups buttermilk
2   cups hot sauce
1   frying chicken, cut-up
4   cups self-rising flour
    Salt and pepper to taste
    Cayenne pepper to taste (optional)
    Vegetable oil for frying

In a large bowl combine the buttermillk and hot sauce. Add the chicken and soak at least 30 minutes or overnight.

Mix together the flour, salt and black pepper. Drain off the chicken and dredge in the flour mixture. Some folks like to sprinkle cayenne over the breaded chicken to give it a bit more bite. It's up to you how you like it.

Heat the vegetable oil to about 330°. Cook the chicken in batches, drain well, and enjoy!

BRUNSWICK STEW

Oh my, people do get stewed up about just what goes into a Brunswick Stew. Originally, I believe that a lot of
squirrel found its way into the pot, and maybe a little pork as well. It varies from pot to pot.
I've limited the pork to bacon drippings and cut the squirrel out altogether, but if you happen to have
a freezer full of squirrel, by all means, throw it in. Rabbit really does work well also. Burgoo is a very similar stew
that is served in Kentucky. Lima beans are requisite in Burgoo. Stews, I believe, are open to interpretation
and some artistic license. If it tastes good, most folks don't care what you call it.

{ SERVES 10. }

1   whole chicken
2   onions, halved
3   ribs celery, roughly chopped
2   carrots, roughly chopped

Water to cover

2   bay leaves

4   sprigs fresh thyme (or 1 teaspoon dried)

4   sprigs parsley

2   teaspoons salt

1   teaspoon white pepper

¼   teaspoon cayenne pepper

Fat from frying 4 slices bacon

1   large onion, chopped

6   cloves garlic, minced

1   bell pepper, chopped

1   cup sliced okra

1   28-ounce can tomatoes

1   tablespoon red wine vinegar

2   cups chicken broth (or more)

Kernels from 2 ears corn

1½   cups fresh butter beans

3   small potatoes, cut in 1-inch pieces

2   teaspoons salt

1   teaspoon black pepper

¼   teaspoon cayenne pepper

1   bay leaf

1   teaspoon thyme leaves

1   teaspoon dried basil

2   teaspoons Worcestershire sauce

*R*inse the chicken and remove the giblets. Place in a pot with the onions, celery, and carrots, and cover with cold water. Bring to a boil along with the seasoning. Reduce the heat to simmer and cook about 40 minutes until tender. Remove the chicken and let cool. Strain the stock and set aside.

Remove the skin from the chicken and pull the meat from the bones. Cool until ready to use.

Fry the bacon in a Dutch oven. Remove the bacon and cook the onion in bacon fat for about 3 minutes. Add the garlic, pepper, and okra, and cook on high heat about 5 minutes. Add the tomatoes and vinegar and cook on high about 10 minutes. Add the stock and bring to a boil. Reduce the heat to medium and add the remaining ingredients. Add more stock if necessary, and adjust the seasoning. Cook until the vegetables are very tender and the liquid is slightly thickened.

Stir in the chicken and heat through. Taste again for seasoning and serve in bowls over rice.

ROAST TURKEY WITH CORN BREAD STUFFING

The quintessential Thanksgiving dinner is very hard to beat. It tastes just as good at other times of the year as well.

{ SERVES 16. }

1   16-pound turkey
½   cup butter, softened
1   tablespoon salt
1   tablespoon black pepper
1   teaspoon cayenne pepper

Preheat the oven to 400°. Remove the giblets from the turkey and rinse. Pat dry. Mix together the butter with the salt and peppers. Rub this inside and outside of the turkey, pushing up under the skin to season the meat. Loosely fill the bird with corn bread stuffing and tie the legs together at the bottom joint. Place breast-side down on a rack fitted inside of a roasting pan and roast for 1 hour.

Baste the bird well with the pan juices and turn down to 350°. Roast for about 3 hours, basting every 20 minutes, and then turn the bird over, breast-side up. Continue roasting until the middle of the stuffing registers 160°.

Remove from the oven and let the bird sit for at least 20 minutes before carving. Serve with Giblet Gravy (see page 188) and cranberry sauce.

CORN BREAD STUFFING

{ SERVES 16. }

1   loaf Corn Light Bread, broken up in rough cubes (see page 216)
1   loaf white bread, broken or torn in rough cubes
4   slices bacon
1   large onion, finely chopped
6   cloves garlic, minced
3   stalks celery, finely chopped
2   carrots, finely chopped
    About 4 cups good chicken stock
1   tablespoon fresh sage, minced (or 2 teaspoons dried crushed)
1   tablespoon chopped parsley
2   scallions, thinly sliced
    Salt and pepper to taste

Place the bread pieces in a large mixing bowl. Set aside. Cook the bacon in a large skillet. Remove the cooked bacon and reserve for another use. Briefly cook the onions, garlic, celery, and carrots in the bacon drippings, just to wilt them. Add to the mixing bowl along with the drippings. Heat the chicken stock to a good boil and pour two thirds of it into the stuffing, along with the remaining ingredients. Mix well and taste. Adjust the seasoning and the consistency with additional stock, as needed. Remember that cooking the stuffing in the bird will moisten it somewhat.

THANKSGIVING NIGHT TURKEY SANDWICH

I feel a little silly giving a recipe for this, but I can't stop talking about turkey until I cover this important topic. Our big Thanksgiving dinner occurs at approximately one o'clock in the afternoon. And, needless to say, it is BIG. But when six o'clock rolls around, something in our bellies cry out from habit for attention. This is what we give our bellies. A roast turkey sandwich. Executed on white bread with mayonnaise, preferably homemade, and garlic salt. That's it. Perfection.

GIBLET GRAVY

3   cups chicken broth from cooking the chicken
1   tablespoon butter
½   onion, minced
1   rib celery, minced
    Giblets from the chicken, cut in small pieces
    Meat pulled from neck bone
1   hard-boiled egg, chopped small
1   teaspoon cornstarch
    Salt and pepper to taste
1   tablespoon chopped parsley
1   tablespoon chopped scallions

Heat the broth in a saucepan to a slow boil and keep warm. Melt the butter in another saucepan to sizzling and cook the onion and celery for 2 or 3 minutes. Add the giblets and neck meat and cook for 3 more minutes. Pour in the broth and bring back to boil. Taste for salt and pepper and adjust the seasoning. Add the egg and let the gravy cook slowly for 20 minutes. Mix the cornstarch with 1 tablespoon of water and stir into the gravy. Bring to a boil. The gravy should thicken slightly. Remove from the heat, stir in the parsley and scallions, and serve.

FRIED TURKEY

Thanksgiving fried turkeys are a big event at Martha's. We usually cook about 50. This is a 2-day affair,
with 4 turkey fryers going non-stop. It frequently seems to rain on those days, but we brave the elements
and get the job done for friends, family, and clients alike.
You may believe this is just a trend, but once you've tried fried turkey I bet you'll be a convert, too.

{ SERVES 8 TO 10. }

1   8- to 12-pound turkey
3   tablespoons salt
1   tablespoon black pepper
1   tablespoon cayenne pepper
1   tablespoon rubbed sage
2   teaspoons dried thyme
1   tablespoon garlic powder
    Peanut or vegetable oil

The day before frying, remove the giblets from the turkey (save them for gravy!). Rinse
and pat dry.

Combine the seasonings. Use a glove to rub the turkey inside and out, pushing as
much flavoring as you can up under the skin without tearing it. Cover the turkey and
refrigerate overnight.

Heat peanut or vegetable oil in a turkey fryer (outside!) to about 325°. Skewer the
turkey on the metal hook, lower carefully into the hot oil, and cook for 30 minutes.
Carefully remove and drain.

This is amazing if you can serve it right away. If you will need to re-heat it, do so
uncovered to crisp up the skin.

TURKEY HASH

Usually served the Friday after Thanksgiving dinner, but so good you really shouldn't wait for just once a year.
You can also make this with chicken.

{ SERVES 8 TO 10. }

¼　cup butter
1　onion, chopped
3　ribs celery, chopped
¼　cup all-purpose flour
4　cups chicken stock
8　small new potatoes, quartered
　　Salt and pepper to taste
　　Dash Worcestershire sauce
4　cups pulled turkey meat

Melt the butter and cook the onion and celery until wilted. Stir in the flour and cook until slightly browned. Stir in the stock and bring to a boil, stirring. Add the new potatoes and turn the heat down to medium. Taste and add salt and pepper. Cook for 20 minutes. Add the turkey meat and cook another 10 minutes. Serve over corn or batter cakes.

ROAST QUAIL WITH BACON

Quail are very plentiful in our woods, and now they're easy to find commercially, so you don't have to rely on a hunter friend. Quail are so small, they really should be cooked quickly or they dry out.

{ SERVES 4. }

8   quail
    Salt and black pepper to taste
1   teaspoon minced fresh thyme
8   slices bacon
1   tablespoon bourbon
2   cups chicken stock

Preheat the oven to 425°. Rinse the quail and pat dry. Season inside and out with salt and pepper (easy on the salt, remember the bacon is mighty salty). Sprinkle thyme leaves over the outside. Wrap one piece of bacon around each quail, making a neat little bundle. Place the birds on a rack fitted into a shallow roasting pan. Roast the birds for about 15 minutes. Remove from the oven and remove the rack with the quail from the roasting pan. Set the roasting pan on top of the stove. Splash in the bourbon, being careful of any flames (it will only flame if directly ignited with flame from a gas burner). Pour in the stock, bring to a boil and reduce until slightly thickened. Serve the quail with mashed potatoes and the sauce over both.

Note: Dove may be cooked the same way. They are especially good prepared this way and cooked on a medium grill.

PAN-BAKED RABBIT

I realize that rabbits do not have wings, but they taste and cook so similarly to chicken that this is the chapter I chose to include them.

Rabbit is a wonderful meat, tasty, healthful, and plentiful. Better for the environment than some forms of livestock, in that they don't take up much space or require a lot of feed in proportion to the meat that they produce.

This is a great hunter–style recipe with a lot of character and heartiness. I like it best in the cold weather months.

{ SERVES 8. }

2	rabbits
¼	cup cider vinegar
	Salt and black pepper to taste
3	tablespoons dry mustard
2	tablespoons all-purpose flour
4	slices bacon
1	onion, chopped
4	cloves garlic, minced
3	cups chicken stock
2	bay leaves

Preheat the oven to 300°. Rinse the rabbits and cut into serving pieces (quarters). Pour the vinegar over and work into the meat. Mix together the salt and pepper, mustard, and flour, and rub all over the rabbit. Cook the bacon in a large Dutch oven and remove when cooked. Add the rabbit and brown evenly on all sides. Add the onion and garlic to the pot about half way through browning the rabbit. Pour in the chicken stock and add the bay leaves. Bring the stock to a boil and cover the pot. Bake for about 1 hour.

Remove the top. Continue cooking for 30 minutes. The meat should be very tender and the stock reduced to a nice sauce. This is great with buttered or mashed turnips or scalloped parsnips.

{ Chapter 9 }

MEATS

While bowls of vegetables, salads, and relishes fill the canvas of a southern table, the meat platter is the energy source around which they revolve. Today, most of us are removed from the agricultural life by only one or two generations. Our grandparents or great grandparents rose with the sun and labored most of the day. They ate as heartily as they worked, and the livestock they fed was the livestock which in turn fed them. Beef, pork, and lamb are all mainstays of our culinary heritage, originally raised and slaughtered responsibly on small farms where children were made aware of the cycle of life and death at an early age. Today, so many of the meats available to us are pumped with hormones and chemicals and slaughtered under circumstances of questionable sanitation. Happily, as the public is made ever more aware, we continue to demand safer and more humane treatment of livestock, in life and death. While the immediate result may raise meat prices, the end results are worth it: immensely tastier meat which is more healthful and a more sound manner in which to treat the earth. After all, we are all God's stewards.

Beef

*B*eef has traditionally been used more for dairy than for butchering in these parts. Remember that the South has never been a really wealthy area except for a very few for a very short while. Cuts of beef tend not to be choice and are frequently extended into stews or meat loaves. These not so choice cuts, however, are usually loaded with flavor. You just have to work on them a bit more.

ROAST BEEF TENDERLOIN

This luxurious cut of beef is a "must" for holiday buffets. So easy to prepare, and certain to impress!

{ SERVES 8 TO 10. }

1   whole beef tenderloin, trimmed (about 3 pounds)
3   tablepoons olive oil
    Kosher salt
    Black pepper
    Granulated garlic

*P*reheat the oven to 400°.
   Place the tenderloin in a roasting pan. Pour the olive oil over the beef and then rub with the spices, seasoning well.
   Roast for 30 minutes for medium rare. Remove from the oven and let rest before slicing.
   Serve with Yeast Rolls (see page 228) and Horseradish Sauce (recipe follows).

HORSERADISH SAUCE

{ MAKES 1½ CUPS. }

1   cup homemade Mayonnaise (see page 29)
½   cup prepared horseradish
½   teaspoons paprika

*I*n a small bowl combine all of the ingredients.
   This may be prepared in advance. Cover and keep refrigerated.

CHICKEN–FRIED STEAK

I asked my mother if she ever ate steak like this as a child, and she responded that this was the only way
she ever ate steak. Times change pretty quickly. There is no chicken involved in this recipe,
but the beef steak is battered and fried as one would a piece of chicken.
Maybe not a nutritionally sound notion for every night of the week, but very beneficial for the soul
now and then, especially on a cold, dark night.

{ SERVES 6. }

2   pounds round steak, cut into 6 thin pieces
1   cup all-purpose flour
½   teaspoon salt
¼   teaspoon black pepper
1   egg, beaten
¼   cup butter

3   tablespoons fat
3   tablespoons all purpose flour
2   cups water
    Salt and pepper to taste

Sprinkle a little salt on the steaks and use a mallet to pound the steaks well. Season 1 cup of flour with the ½ teaspoon of salt and ¼ teaspoon pepper and dredge the steaks in this. Dip them in the beaten egg and dredge again in the seasoned flour. Heat the butter in a heavy skillet. Add the steaks and cook over medium high heat about 1½ minutes per side, longer for thicker cuts. Don't overcook or they'll get tough. Remove the steaks from the pan and keep warm while you make gravy.

You should have some fat left in the pan after you remove the steaks. If you don't, add a little more butter so that you have about 3 tablespoons of fat in the pan. Stir in 3 tablespoons of flour and cook, stirring, until it browns. Pour in the water, stirring, and bring to a boil. Reduce the heat and cook about 5 or 10 minutes. Season with salt and pepper and serve with the steaks. Mashed potatoes are a natural with this meal.

FLANK STEAK

Flank steak is one of the tastiest cuts of meat, but can be tough if not prepared correctly.
Two tricks: cook it quickly on high heat, and cut it against the grain.

This marinade is Asian–inspired. It would also be delicious prepared with the Chipotle BBQ Sauce (see
page 181) or the marinade for Marinated Grilled Lamb (see page 204).

{ S E R V E S 6 . }

1	flank steak (about 1½ pounds)
½	cup soy sauce
2	teaspoons fresh minced garlic
2	teaspoons fresh minced ginger
	Juice of 2 limes
1	tablespoon sesame oil

Rinse the steaks and pat dry. Place in a Pyrex baking dish with the remaining ingredients. Marinate 30 for minutes to 2 hours.

Prepare a grill to medium. Cook the steaks for 10 to 15 minutes, about 5 to 8 minutes per side. Slice thinly on the diagonal and serve with peanut sauce.

POT ROAST

I like my pot roast falling apart with lots of yummy vegetables and some good gravy in the pot. This will deliver.

{ S E R V E S A B O U T 1 2 . }

3	slices bacon
5	pounds chuck roast
2	cups all-purpose flour
1	teaspoon salt
½	teaspoon black pepper
½	teaspoon dried thyme
1	quart beef stock
6	onions, peeled and quartered
8	potatoes, cut in large cubes

12   carrots, peeled and cut in large pieces
½   cup red wine (optional)
     Additional stock

Preheat the oven to 300°. Cook the bacon in a Dutch oven or skillet and remove when done, leaving the drippings. Mix the flour with the seasonings on a plate. Rinse the roast and dredge in the flour. Brown the roast in the bacon grease. Pour in the stock. If the stock is not very flavorful, you should add a little salt and pepper to taste. Cover the roast and bake for 3 hours, until the roast is exquisitely tender. Add the vegetables, coating them with the pan juices. If most of the stock has cooked out, add a little more, or about ½ cup of red wine. Cook uncovered for 1 more hour.

FRIED CALF'S LIVER

You love it or you hate. I love it, especially like this. Calf's liver is prepared in the same fashion as the steaks.

{ SERVES 6. }

6   slices calf's liver
1   cup buttermilk
½   teaspoon salt
¼   teaspoon black pepper
1   cup all-purpose flour
6   strips bacon
2   eggs

Rinse the liver and soak in the buttermilk for an hour. Mix the salt and pepper with the flour and set on plate. Cook the bacon in a heavy skillet and remove when done. Dredge the liver in the flour. Dip in the beaten egg and dredge in the flour again. Cook the liver in the bacon fat for 4 minutes per side. Serve with Glazed Onions (see page 121) and crumble the bacon on top.

MEAT LOAF

Meat loaf can be as wonderful as the maker. Put some love into it, and your meat loaf, your friends,
and your family will all love you back.

{ SERVES 8 TO 10. }

2	pounds ground chuck
1	pound pork sausage
1	onion, chopped
6	cloves garlic, minced
2	ribs celery, chopped
1	red bell pepper, chopped
1½	teaspoons salt
½	teaspoon black pepper
¼	teaspoon cayenne pepper
1	teaspoon dried oregano
1	teaspoon dried sage
⅔	cup tomato purée
⅓	cup Dijon mustard
2	teaspoons Worcestershire sauce
1	egg
½	cup breadcrumbs

Use a large mixing bowl to mix everything together. If you use your hands, it's a good idea to wear rubber gloves. Form into 2 rounds or pack into loaf pans. Bake at 400° for about 1 hour until completely cooked through.

Serve with Brown Gravy (recipe follows).

BROWN GRAVY FOR MEAT LOAF

Use a good canned or frozen stock.

{ SERVES 8 TO 10. }

3   tablespoons butter
3   tablespoons all-purpose flour
2   cups rich beef stock
    Dash soy sauce
    Salt and pepper to taste

Heat the butter in a saucepan and stir in the flour. Cook, stirring constantly, until lightly browned. Stir in the stock, bring to a boil, and simmer for 15 minutes. Add soy sauce, salt, and pepper.

SPICED ROUND

In an odd culinary digression for Nashville, German meat-packers set up shop in town in the mid-eighteen hundreds and introduced the mid-South to Spiced Round, a round of beef that is generously larded throughout with strips of spiced pork fat, and then aged in brine. The meat is purchased after brining to be cooked at home, as you would a corned beef. Nashville's spiced rounds have been rather famous—especially around holiday times—for generations, although you don't see them as frequently now as when my parents were young.

My immediate family didn't often cook spiced rounds. We didn't have to because Aunt Sue always did. I remember them at her house for Christmas and New Year's. She purchased one with a lot of mustard in the pork fat, creating perfect yellow circles in a pale pink roast. Quite exotic if not frightening to a small child, yet I, of course, had to eat it, to the dismay of sisters and cousins alike. Seeing that much glorified fat is a bit odd to modern American minds, but it is, truly, delicious. The roast itself is so lean and briny that the fat rather balances it. What can I say. You simply have to try it.

Here's how to cook a spiced round once you get it home.

Soak the spiced round in cold water for 1 hour. Remove the round from the water. Place on a rack in the bottom of a very large pot. Wrap the roast a couple of times around with heavy foil to preserve the tightly formed shape. Place the round on the rack and cover with cold water. Stir in 1 cup of brown sugar. Bring to a boil, reduce to a simmer, and cook for 15 minutes per pound. Remove and let cool. Rewrap in more foil and chill in the refrigerator. Slice thinly and serve cold with mustard if desired.

BEEF STEW

Hearty and hale, beef stew takes the edge off the cold and smooths out the bumps of the day.
This gets better the second day.

{ SERVES ABOUT 12. }

1   cup all-purpose flour
1   teaspoon salt
½   teaspoon black pepper
4   pounds beef chuck, cut into 10-inch cubes
3   tablespoons vegetable oil
1   tablespoon tomato paste
3   cups beef stock
1   teaspoon dried thyme
1   teaspoon dried oregano
1   bay leaf
½   cup red wine
    Additional salt and pepper to taste
3   tablespoons butter
1   large onion, chopped
6   cloves garlic, minced
2   carrots, cut in 1-inch pieces
6   new potatoes, quartered
2   medium turnips, peeled and cut in 1-inch pieces
1   pint mushrooms, quartered
    Salt and pepper to taste

Mix the flour, salt, and pepper together on a plate. Dredge the cubed beef in the flour. Heat the vegetable oil in a Dutch oven and brown the meat on all sides. Stir in the tomato paste and cook for a couple of minutes. Pour in the stock, herbs, and wine. Taste the liquid and add salt and pepper if necessary. Bring to a boil, stir, and reduce the heat to low. Cover and cook for 1 hour and 30 minutes.

Heat the butter in a large skillet and sauté the onion, garlic, and carrots for about 5 minutes. Remove the cover from the stew and stir in the sautéed vegetables along with the potatoes and turnips. Add more stock, if necessary, to cover all of the vegetables. Cook for 30 minutes, then stir in the mushrooms. Adjust the seasoning and cook for 30 minutes more.

Serve in bowls or over corn cakes.

SHEPHERD'S PIE

This is a real family pleaser. Great for a cold winter's night. The potatoes soak up some of the meaty juice…mmmm! Divine!

{ SERVES 4 TO 6. }

FOR THE MEAT:

1   pound ground lamb
1   yellow onion, chopped
3   carrots, chopped
5   cloves garlic, minced
1   small can chopped tomatoes
½   teaspoon cinnamon
1   teaspoon cumin
1   tablespoons cider vinegar
1   tablespoon brown sugar

In a large skillet brown the lamb with the onion, carrots, and garlic. Pour off as much fat as you can. Add the remaining ingredients, Stir and cook about 20 minutes.
   Meanwhile cook the potatoes.

FOR THE POTATOES:

1   pound Yukon gold potatoes
4   tablespoons butter
1   cup milk
    Salt and pepper

Cook the potatoes in boiling salted water until quite soft. Drain well and mash with the milk, butter, salt and pepper to taste.
   Preheat the oven to 400°.
   Spoon the meat mixture into a baking dish. Top with the potatoes and bake for about 30 minutes, until the potatoes begin to brown.

MEAT PIE

You can make this up in an instant with leftover stew, and everyone will think you have done something
really special. You have, of course, but with a casual nonchalance that lends an attractive air of mystery
to your person. In other words, folks will be amazed.

This savory pie is yummy and satisfying with any juicy, slow-cooked meat such as pot roast or beef brisket.
I like to make pies from stew, because I like all of the vegetables.

{ S ERVES 8 . }

6   cups beef stew
1   recipe Pie Crust (see page 268)
1   egg mixed with 2 tablespoons milk

 *P*reheat the oven to 375°. If the stew is very thick, just spoon about 6 cups of it into
a baking dish. If the stew is a little runny, use a slotted spoon to leave some of the
juice behind.
    Roll out the pastry and cut a little wider than the baking dish. Cover the stew and
crimp the edges. If you have some dough left over, you can use that to cut out leaves,
hearts, or other designs to top your pie. Stir the egg and milk together and use a pastry brush to paint it over the pastry. If you are using any cut-outs, place them on top of
the painted dough and paint these, as well. Make a few slits in the pastry and bake for
20 to 30 minutes, until the pastry is browned and the stew is bubbly.

ROAST LAMB

Roast lamb can be really horrible: stringy, gray, and dry. That said, this lamb is juicy and flavorful, with a crispy
outside and and a little pink inside. The potatoes are divine.

{ S ERVES ABOUT 8 . }

1   leg of lamb, about 5 pounds
½   cup butter
6   cloves garlic, cut in slivers
1   teaspoon salt
½   teaspoon black pepper
    Leaves from 2 sprigs fresh rosemary
10   new potatoes, scrubbed and cut in halves

$\mathcal{P}$reheat the oven to 400°. Make a paste of the butter and seasonings, and rub all over the lamb. Place in a roasting pan and cook for 15 minutes. Turn the oven down to 350° and cook the lamb for 1 hour. Stir the potatoes into the pan juices and cook at least 30 more minutes, until the potatoes are cooked through and the lamb is cooked to your desire, about 145° for medium. Remove the lamb from the pan and keep the potatoes warm. Let the lamb sit outside of the oven for at least 10 minutes before you slice it. If you don't, all of the juices will spill out and onto your cutting board. Slice the meat and place on a platter with the potatoes around. Pour any pan juices over the lamb and serve.

It is most traditional to serve roast lamb with a mint jelly of which, I have to tell you, I am not too fond. I prefer to serve roast lamb with Southern Fried Apples (recipe follows) or a nice chutney. If you miss the mint flavor, try stirring some roughly chopped mint into the apples.

SOUTHERN FRIED APPLES

These go with a thousand things, every meat you imagine.

{ SERVES ABOUT 8. }

10 tart young apples, unpeeled, sliced
¾   cup firmly packed brown sugar
¼   cup butter (or 3 tablespoons butter and 1 tablespoon bacon fat)
1   cup water
½   teaspoon ground cinnamon

$\mathcal{P}$lace everything together in a heavy skillet and stir until the sugar dissolves. Cover and cook over low heat for 20 minutes. Remove the cover and cook 5 or 10 more minutes until the liquid is almost all cooked out. Serve warm.

MARINATED GRILLED LAMB

I think folks are intimidated by lamb, or they believe it will taste gamey. The pasture grazed lamb I buy is deliciously mild, and the boneless leg is perfect for the grill. Try it just once, and I bet you'll want to make it again.

{ SERVES ABOUT 6. }

¼   cup olive oil
     Juice and zest of 2 lemons
 2   teaspoons minced fresh garlic
 1   tablespoon fresh rosemary leaves
 1   teaspoon salt
½   teaspoon black pepper

 1   boneless leg of lamb, butterflied open and trimmed of excess fat

In a small bowl combine the olive oil, lemon juice and zest, garlic, rosemary, salt, and pepper.

Place the lamb in a Pyrex baking dish. Pour the marinade over the lamb, and refrigerate for at least an hour or overnight.

Heat a grill to medium. Let the excess marinade drip from the lamb, and place it on the grill. Cook a total of about 30 minutes, turning occasionally for medium rare.

Serve with Mint and Parlsey Pesto (recipe follows).

MINT AND PARSLEY PESTO

So delicious with so many things! We spread on a sandwich with goat cheese, and serve it with grilled chicken. The herbs happen to be a perfect match for lamb.

{ MAKES 1 QUART. }

 1   cup packed mint leaves
 1   cup packed flat leaf parsley leaves (most stems removed)
1½   teaspoons minced fresh garlic
¼   cup olive oil
 2   tablespoons crumbled feta cheese
 1   tablespoon freshly grated Parmesan cheese

2   teaspoons capers
½   teaspoon red pepper flakes
    Juice and zest of 1 lemon

*I*n a food processer combine everything and process until almost smooth. Serve at room temperature.

Pork

*S*outherners probably eat more pork than anyone else in the country. When I went to culinary school in New York, I sometimes felt like pork was considered a lower class of meat. This, of course, is absurd. Pork has enormous flavor, cooks beautifully, and can be one of the healthiest meats you could eat, depending on the cut. Pork popularity is definitely on the upswing, however. Pork has proudly found its way onto the menu of many a swank restaurant, and its virtues are being extolled by nutritionists, economists, and environmentalists alike. Let's hear it for pork.

PORK TENDERLOIN

This cut of pork is so delicious — it's really hard to mess up! Just don't over-cook it, and you can't go wrong.

{ S E R V E S 4 T O 6 . }

1   package with 2 pork tenderloin, rinsed and trimmed of silver skin
1   can chipotle peppers with adobo sauce, puréed in food processer

*C*ut the tenderloins in half lengthwise and place in a Pyrex baking dish. Pour the pureed peppers over the pork. Wearing gloves, rub the peppers completely over each piece of pork. Let marinate for 1 hour or overnight in the refrigerator.

Heat a grill to medium. Allow excess peppers to drip off the pork and place on the prepared grill. Cook for a total of 15 to 20 minutes, turning occasionally, until medium (a little juicy and pink in the middle). Serve with Black-Eyed Pea Salsa (see page 40) and Guacamole (see page 41).

SLOW–BAKED PORK CHOPS

A great meal for company. It gives you almost an hour to relax and will hold in a warm oven well after that.

{ SERVES 8. }

8   thick pork chops
1   cup all-purpose flour
1   teaspoon salt
½   teaspoon black pepper
3   tablespoons butter
2   tart apples, cored and cut in thick slices
2   onions, cut in thick slices
1   cup chicken stock
1   teaspoon minced fresh thyme leaves

Preheat the oven to 325°. Rinse the pork chops and pat dry. Mix the flour, salt, and pepper together on a plate. Heat the butter in a Dutch oven or deep skillet and brown the pork chops about 4 minutes per side. Stir in the apples and onions and cook about 3 minutes. Stir in the stock and thyme. Cover and bake for 45 minutes to an hour, checking occasionally to make sure the stock has not cooked out, until the pork is very tender.

Heaven with mashed potatoes.

PAN–FRIED PORK CHOPS

Tasty, tasty!

{ SERVES 4. }

8   thin-sliced pork chops, 2 per person
½   cup all-purpose flour
½   teaspoon salt
½   teaspoon black pepper
3   tablespoons butter

Rinse the pork chops and pat dry. Mix the flour, salt, and pepper together on a plate and dredge the chops in this. Heat the butter in a skillet and fry the chops about 5 minutes per side. If you'd like a gravy, make as with Chicken Fried Steak, (see page

195). A strong vinegary pickle is also good, such as chow chow or green tomato pickle or corn relish.

Mama usually serves applesauce with these.

BARBECUED PORK SHOULDER

A great meal for a summer party and really fool–proofed by doing most of the cooking prior to the grilling.

{ SERVES 6 TO 8. }

1   3- to 4-pound pork shoulder
    Water to cover
1   tablespoon salt
1   tablespoon black pepper
3   cayenne peppers

2   teaspoons salt
2   teaspoons black pepper
2   cloves garlic, minced
1   teaspoon cayenne pepper
¼   cup vegetable oil

Have the butcher butterfly the pork shoulder. Rinse it and place in a large pot. Cover with water and add the salt and peppers. Bring to a slow boil and cook for 1 hour.

Have the grill lit and cooking at a medium heat. Remove the pork from the water and pat dry.

Combine all of the remaining ingredients and rub into the meat. Place the meat over medium-low coals, off-center from the strongest heat, and cook about 30 minutes, turning now and then. Most people like for at least part of outside to get quite crispy. My sisters and I always fought over the crispy pieces.

Remove from the grill and let sit for about 10 minutes before slicing and serving with your choice of barbecue sauce. Following are two I like.

RIBS

This is more about method than seasoning. I think you'll like how this works!

{ SERVES 2 TO 4. }

1   package ribs (about 3 pounds)
2   tablespoons salt
1   tablespoon black pepper
1   teaspoon cayenne pepper
1   to 2 cups Red Barbecue Sauce (recipe follows)

Remove the ribs from the package. Rinse well. Place in a large pot and cover with water. Add 1 tablespoon of salt and bring to a boil. Reduce the heat to simmer and cook for 20 to 30 minutes, until quite tender.

Prepare a grill to medium. Drain the ribs and pat dry. Rub the ribs with salt and peppers. Cook on the grill a total of about 20 minutes, 10 minutes per side, basting occasionally with barbecue sauce. Serve with additional sauce.

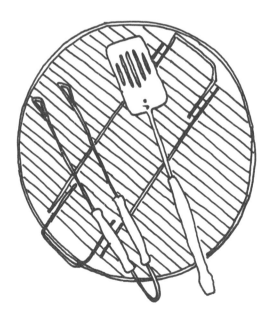

RED BARBECUE SAUCE

¼ cup vegetable oil
½ onion, coarsely grated
6 cloves garlic, minced
2 fresh cayenne peppers, minced
1 cup ketchup
¾ cup vinegar
¼ teaspoon ground cinnamon
½ teaspoon celery seed
½ teaspoon black pepper

Heat the vegetable oil in a heavy saucepan and add the onion, garlic, and cayenne. Cook, stirring, for 5 minutes. Add the remaining ingredients and bring to a boil, stirring occasionally. Taste for seasoning. Simmer for 10 minutes, then let cool.

VINEGAR BARBECUE SAUCE

2 tablespoons oil
¾ cup white vinegar
2 tablespoons Worcestershire sauce
1 tablespoon firmly packed brown sugar
½ onion, grated
   Juice of 1 lemon
1 teaspoon cayenne pepper (or more)

Mix everything together and let sit for at least 1 hour, or—even better—overnight.

BREAKFAST SAUSAGE

This is really easy to make and very, very tasty. How nice to know exactly what's in it as well!

4   pounds ground pork
6   cloves garlic, minced
1   tablespoon salt
1   tablespoon red pepper flakes
1½ teaspoons black pepper
1½ tablespoons fresh sage, minced

Place all ingredients in a bowl and mix together very thoroughly. Shape into patties and cook in a skillet over medium heat until browned and cooked through.

If this recipe makes more than you will use in one meal, you may shape your patties, wrap, and freeze them. Use within one month to avoid freezer burn.

SAUSAGE GRAVY

A real luxury which I rarely allow myself. This will serve as breakfast and lunch in one.

1   pound bulk sausage meat
2   tablespoons all-purpose flour
4   cups milk, heated

Brown the sausage meat in a skillet on medium high, crumbling the sausage as it cooks. Remove the meat, reduce the heat to medium low, and stir in the flour, scraping browned bits up from the pan. Stir and cook for 3 minutes. Pour in the warm milk, stirring out any lumps. Raise the heat and cook on medium, stirring occasionally, for 15 minutes. Add the sausage back to the pan and heat through. Serve over warm, split buttermilk biscuits.

{ *Chapter 10* }

BREADS

I love to cook all different types of bread, bringing plates of biscuits and muffins, or pans of corn bread to the table. So many of us have grown accustomed to packaged breads and rolls. While they do serve to mop up the juices on your plate, they can't possibly compete with the satisfaction of freshly made breads. Packaged breads can't give your home the sweet, warm smell of fresh rolls or corn bread in the oven, and none of them could possibly give the flavor of scratch-made goods. Waffles in the toaster, pancakes in the microwave, biscuits from a can, I guess they all have their place in this absurdly busy society that we have managed to create for ourselves, but a few nights, maybe just one night a week or one night a month, do yourself a favor and take twenty minutes to make up some biscuits or mix up some corn bread. And if you really have some time, try a batch of yeast rolls or honey whole wheat bread. You can't imagine the magic that happens with a package of yeast, some dry goods, and a pair of hands. It's more than chemistry.

CORN PONES

The South's romance with cornmeal is centuries old and still going strong. I always try to use stone-ground meal from a small mill. The sweet flavor of corn almost mystically shines when a good meal is cooked. There are probably a hundred types of corn bread flavored with vegetables, herbs, and cheese. Corn breads may be baked or fried. Pones are usually started on top of a hot griddle, which is then popped into a hot oven. Crispy outside, tender in the middle. A "Johnny Cake" is the grandaddy of American corn pones—what the Native Americans taught European settlers to make. The recipes I have seen are quite similar to the corn pone recipe here.

Mamma and Daddy liked to eat these with sorghum. A little stout for me,
I like them with butter and sweet locally made honey.

{ Makes about 10 small pones. }

1	cup coarse white cornmeal
½	teaspoon salt
½	cup water
1	tablespoon butter, melted
¼	teaspoon baking soda
½	cup buttermilk

Preheat the oven to 450°. Mix the meal with the salt in a medium bowl. Bring the water to a boil and pour into the meal mixture. Add the melted butter. Dissolve the soda in the buttermilk and add to the meal. Form into balls and flatten out on a hot greased griddle. Bake in the oven until browned on one side. Turn and brown on the other.

Serve hot with butter and sorghum for breakfast, or with greens or fried fish.

CRACKLING PONES

Cracklings are made from pork skin and give this bread an unforgettable rich flavor. They're still sold in a lot of neighborhood grocery stores, or ask your butcher about them.

{ Makes about 16 pones. }

1	cup water
2	cups coarse cornmeal
1	teaspoon salt
1	cup cracklings

¼ teaspoon baking soda
¾ cup buttermilk

$\mathcal{P}$reheat the oven to 425°. Boil the water and pour over the cornmeal in a large bowl. Stir. Add the salt and cracklings. Dissolve the soda in the buttermilk and stir into the mixture, mixing thoroughly. Form balls and flatten onto a hot greased griddle. Bake until brown on one side, turn, and brown on the other.

SWEET POTATO PONES

The rich sweet potatoes and cornmeal really complement each other. You may substitute winter squash for the sweet potato to vary the flavor. Try roasting 1 winter squash and mashing the pulp to get about 1 quart.

With sweet potatoes or squash, these are substantial enough to serve as a starch with dinner. Excellent with pork or turkey.

Try heating any leftovers for breakfast with honey or sorghum.

{ Makes about 16 pones. }

4   sweet potatoes
1   egg
2   cups stone-ground cornmeal
1   teaspoon salt
½   teaspoon baking soda
1   tablespoon shortening, melted
½   cup buttermilk (about)

$\mathcal{P}$reheat the oven to 350°. Bake the sweet potatoes in their skins for about 45 minutes until very soft. Peel and mash while still hot. Beat in the egg, then stir in everything but the buttermilk. Add just enough buttermilk to make a stiff batter. Form into small balls and flatten slightly onto a hot greased griddle. Bake for about 30 minutes. Serve hot with butter.

HOT WATER CORN BREAD

These are so good. They're even better if you use a quality stone ground cornmeal from a small mill.
This is a fine example of sublime simplicity.

{ MAKES ABOUT 12 SMALL PIECES OF CORN BREAD. }

2   cups good cornmeal
½   teaspoon salt
2   cups boiling water
    Vegetable oil

Stir the cornmeal and salt together in a large bowl. Heat about ½-inch of oil in a skillet. Pour the hot water over the meal and stir together to a thick mash. Drop by spoonfuls into the hot oil and fry until golden brown all over. Drain on a clean brown paper bag and sprinkle with more salt.

CORN LIGHT BREAD

This is another one of Mama's recipes, but I have cut way back on the sugar which I think makes it a
more well rounded bread. The texture of this is like a dense bread, perfect for slicing.
It makes a great corn bread stuffing and is divine with barbecued pork shoulder.

{ SERVES 6 TO 8. }

2   cups stone-ground cornmeal
¼   cup sugar
½   teaspoon salt
1   teaspoon baking soda
1   cup buttermilk
2   tablespoons shortening

Preheat the oven to 350°. Grease and flour a medium loaf pan. Mix the dry ingredients together in a mixing bowl. Stir in the buttermilk. Melt the shortening and add, mixing well. Pour into the prepared loaf pan and bake about 40 minutes, until cooked through and browned .

SPOON BREAD

So good. Passing the spoon bread around the table just seems to bring a family closer together.

{ SERVES 8. }

1½ cups water
1½ tablespoons shortening, melted
  1 cup cornmeal
  3 whole eggs, well beaten
  1 cup milk
  1 tablespoon baking powder
  ¼ teaspoon salt

In a saucepan heat the water with the shortening. Bring to a boil and pour over the meal in a medium bowl. Stir until blended and cool. Stir in the eggs, milk, salt, and baking powder. Mix thoroughly and pour into a well greased 8-inch baking dish or cake pan. Bake for 30 minutes until firm. Serve in the baking dish with butter.

BUTTERMILK CORN BREAD

A classic recipe. Very fast and simple. You'll wonder why you don't make it more often.

{ SERVES 8 TO 10. }

2 cups cornmeal
1 teaspoon salt
1 teaspoon baking soda
2 cups buttermilk
2 eggs
1 tablespoon bacon fat or butter

Preheat the oven to 375°. Mix the dry ingredients in a large bowl. Pour in the buttermilk and beat in the eggs. Melt the fat in a cast-iron skillet. Pour in the batter and bake in the skillet for 20 to 25 minutes, until risen and browned.

FRESH CORN BATTER CAKES

Ella Hayes (Miss Ella to me) fried these for the whole family and all of their guests in their house on Monteagle Mountain straight through her eighty-seventh year. She would cook the bacon first and use the drippings for cooking the corn cakes. That could get anyone out of bed.

{ MAKES ABOUT 10 CAKES. }

2   to 4 ears sweet corn
2   cups all-purpose flour
1   teaspoon baking powder
1   teaspoon salt
1   tablespoon butter
1   cup milk
1   egg

If the corn seems really tough, you can boil it a few minutes first. With good, sweet corn there's no need. Scrape the corn from the cob to get 1 cup. Sift together the flour, baking powder, and salt. Melt the butter and stir in along with the milk. Beat the egg and mix in. Stir in the grated corn. Cook on a lightly greased griddle on top of the stove, turning once. Serve hot.

BUTTERMILK PANCAKES

The ultimate snowy-day breakfast.

{ MAKES ABOUT 12 CAKES. }

2½ cups all-purpose flour
2½ teaspoons baking powder

½   teaspoon salt
2   teaspoons sugar
2   tablespoons melted butter
1   egg
1½ cups buttermilk
    Vegetable oil for frying

ift together the dry ingredients and place in a mixing bowl. In a separate bowl, mix together the melted butter, egg and buttermilk. Make a well in the center of the dry ingredients and whisk in the wet, just to incorporate.

Heat a griddle or non-stick pan to medium. Add just enough oil to coat the bottom of the pan. Ladle 2 ounces (⅛ cup) of batter for each pancake. Cook until the edges begin to brown and the center bubbles up. Flip and brown the other side. Serve hot with butter and syrup.

JOHNNY CAKE

Some people say that "Johnny" is actually a profoundly southern pronunciation of the word "journey."
These were called "journey" cakes because they held well when packed for a journey.

Boasting both cornmeal and flour, Johnny cakes are very satisfying and good for breakfast, lunch, or dinner.

{ MAKES ABOUT 8 CAKES. }

1	cup buttermilk
1	egg, beaten
½	teaspoon salt
2	teaspoons sugar
½	teaspoon baking soda
6	tablespoons cornmeal
3	tablespoons all-purpose flour

ombine the ingredients in a medium bowl and mix until blended. Spoon the mixture into a hot griddle and cook each side until crispy brown.

BATTER BREAD

This has a great texture. Good with stew or a bit of gravy. It's also nice with butter and sorghum for breakfast.

{ SERVES 8. }

1   cup water
1   cup milk
1   cup cornmeal
2   tablespoons cold boiled rice
1   teaspoon salt
1   tablespoon melted butter
2   eggs, well beaten
1   teaspoon baking powder

Preheat the oven to 350°. Boil the water together with the milk. Pour over the cornmeal and rice. Add the remaining ingredients and pour into a greased baking dish. Bake until firm and serve very hot.

POPOVERS

Beautiful and delicious. I particularly like popovers with pot roast.

{ MAKES ABOUT 6 POPOVERS. }

½   teaspoon salt
1   cup all-purpose flour
1   cup buttermilk
2   eggs
2   teaspoons melted shortening

Preheat the oven to 425° and heat a greased popover pan. Mix the salt and flour in a medium bowl. Add the milk slowly, stirring out any lumps. Beat the eggs lightly and add to the batter. Add the melted shortening and beat very well. Fill the greased popover tins half full. Bake for 30 minutes.

WHOLE WHEAT BISCUITS

A pleasant change of pace, a little heavier than your basic biscuit. Particularly nice with honey.

{ MAKES ABOUT 18 BISCUITS. }

3   cups whole wheat flour
1   teaspoon salt
4   teaspoons baking powder
3   tablespoons shortening
1   cup cream

Preheat the oven to 425°. Sift the dry ingredients into a large bowl. Work in the shortening with the tips of your fingers. Quickly stir the cream in, making a soft dough. Roll 1/2-inch thick, cut, and place on a greased baking sheet. Bake about 10 minutes.

BUTTERMILK BISCUITS

The real thing. The shortening makes them bake up light, and the buttermilk gives great flavor and silky texture.

{ MAKES 18 TO 20 SMALL BISCUITS. }

2   cups all-purpose flour
½   teaspoon salt
¾   teaspoon baking powder
½   teaspoon baking soda
1   heaping tablespoon shortening (the size of a small egg)
¼   cup buttermilk (or clabber cream)

Preheat the oven to 425°. Sift together the dry ingredients in a large bowl. Work in the shortening with just your fingertips until it resembles cornmeal. Add the buttermilk or clabber, just enough to make a stiff dough. Knead the dough lightly, but do not over work. Roll or pat out on a floured board to ¼-inch to ½-inch thickness. Cut into rounds and place on an ungreased cookie sheet. Bake for 12 to 15 minutes, until lightly browned. Serve hot with butter .

CINNAMON BISCUIT SCRAPS

I used to live for biscuit scraps as a little girl. A fun treat. They smell marvelous while baking.

Roll out the leftover scraps of biscuit dough as thinly as possible. Spread the dough with softened butter and sprinkle with cinnamon and sugar mixed together. Roll the dough up jelly roll style and slice off 1-inch pieces. Place on a greased cookie sheet and bake at 400° degrees for about 10 minutes.

SCALLION BISCUITS

This is our house bread at Martha's at the Plantation. The butter, cream, and eggs not only add flavor, they make the biscuit hold much better.

{ MAKES ABOUT 1 DOZEN BISCUITS. }

1½ cups all-purpose flour
 1   tablespoon baking powder
½   teaspoon salt
10 ounces (2½ sticks) butter, diced
 2   eggs, beaten
 2   tablespoons cream
 1   scallion, thinly sliced

In a food processor mix the dry ingredients. Add the diced butter and pulse. Mix in the eggs and cream. Add flour as needed to get a workable dough.

Preheat the oven to 375.

On a floured work surface, roll out the dough to ½-inch thick. Cut in rounds. Place 1 inch apart on a parchment lined baking sheet. Bake for 10 minutes, until golden brown.

SWEET POTATO BISCUITS

These taste very rich and sweat potato–ey, thanks to the baking of the sweet potatoes, which intensifies their flavor.

{ MAKES ABOUT 16 BISCUITS. }

2   sweet potatoes
2   cups all-purpose flour
3   tablespoons baking powder
½   teaspoon baking soda
¾   teaspoon salt
3   tablespoons firmly packed brown sugar
1   teaspoon ground ginger
¼   teaspoon grated nutmeg
½   cup butter, melted
⅔   cup buttermilk
¼   cup raw sugar

Preheat the oven to 350°. Bake the sweet potatoes in their skins for about 30 minutes, until very soft. Peel and mash while still hot.

Turn the oven up to 400°. Sift together the dry ingredients and set aside. Place the mashed sweet potato in a mixing bowl and beat in the melted butter. Add the flour mixture and then the buttermilk. Don't over mix. The dough will be quite tacky. Pat down the dough to ½ inch on a floured board and cut out with a floured biscuit cutter. Sprinkle the tops with the raw sugar. Place on a greased cookie sheet and bake for about 20 minutes until browned. If the bottom begins to be too brown before the tops, turn the oven to broil and watch carefully until the tops are nicely browned. Serve with butter and sorghum or honey.

CORNMEAL WAFFLES

I love the texture of these. The outside gets really crispy and soaks up lots of maple syrup.
These are also great for dinner with beef or turkey hash.

{ MAKES ABOUT 6 WAFFLES. }

2 cups cornmeal
½ teaspoon baking soda
1 teaspoon salt
1 teaspoon baking powder
2 teaspoons sugar
½ cup all-purpose flour
2 eggs
2 cups buttermilk
½ cup vegetable oil

Mix together the dry ingredients in a large bowl. Beat the eggs, combine with the buttermilk, and mix into the dry ingredients, stirring the oil in last. Pour the batter into a preheated waffle iron and cook until brown.

WAFFLES

My sisters and I waged a continual battle over waffles with our grandmother, who believed that we were eating our waffles under-done. "Anemic looking," she called them. A true waffle lover herself, our anemic looking waffles upset her to no end. She shook her head in disgust and took her own waffle so brown that it was almost burnt. We complained that they scratched the tops of our mouths. Luckily there were always plenty of waffles to suit everyone.

{ MAKES ABOUT 8 LARGE WAFFLES. }

1 teaspoon salt
2 tablespoons cornmeal
1 teaspoon baking soda
1 teaspoon baking powder
4 cups all-purpose flour
2 eggs, beaten
2 cups buttermilk
2 tablespoons shortening, added last

ift the dry ingredients in a large bowl and set aside. Beat well the eggs and butter-milk in a separate bowl. Make a well in the dry ingredients and pour in the egg-butter-milk mixture. Pour in the melted shortening to combine. Pour into a preheated waffle iron and bake until golden. Turn onto a warm platter and brush with melted butter.

APPLE BREAKFAST CAKE

A very pretty breakfast cake for a special weekend. It can be made ahead and wrapped in foil to reheat, but it's not quite the same as serving it fresh.

{ SERVES 10. }

1	cup milk
⅓	cup butter
⅔	cup sugar
1	teaspoon salt
1	envelope yeast
2	eggs
	All-purpose flour
5	tart apples
¼	cup sugar
½	teaspoon ground cinnamon
2	tablespoons currants
¼	cup butter, melted

cald the milk and mix together with shortening, sugar, and salt. Let cool to tepid and stir in the yeast. When the yeast has foamed, after about 5 minutes, beat in the eggs and enough flour to make a soft dough. Cover and let rise for 1 hour.

Beat down thoroughly, cover, and let rise again. Spread into a pan greased with shortening. Brush the top with melted butter.

Peel and core the apples and slice into eighths. Press the apple slices into the cake in 2 rows. Mix the sugar and cinnamon together and sprinkle over the top, along with the currants. Cover lightly and let rise another hour.

Bake in a preheated 350° oven for 30 minutes.

HONEY WHOLE WHEAT BREAD

Mama started making this bread when I was a preteen. I used to go on long winter walks through the hills around Radnor Lake and come home to find a fire in the kitchen fireplace, the tea kettle on the stove, and the bread fresh out of the oven with a knife and butter waiting. Definitely worth coming home to.

{ MAKES 2 MEDIUM LOAVES. }

3   cups plus 1 cup whole wheat flour
½   cup nonfat dry milk
1   tablespoon salt
2   packages dry yeast
3   cups water
½   cup honey
2   tablespoons vegetable oil
3   cups all-purpose flour (or more as needed)

Grease 2 9x5-inch loaf pans. Combine 3 cups of whole wheat flour, dry milk, salt and yeast together in a large bowl. Heat the water, honey, and vegetable oil over low heat to just warm. Pour the warm liquid over the dry ingredients and mix with an electric mixer for about 3 minutes.

Add the additional whole wheat flour and all-purpose flour and stir in by hand. Turn out onto a floured board and knead for 5 minutes. Place the dough in a greased bowl. Cover and let rise until doubles in bulk, about 45 minutes to 1 hour.

Punch down the dough and divide in half. Using a rolling pin, roll each half into a rectangle. Roll up like a jelly roll, starting from one of the shorter ends, and place the rolled dough in greased loaf pans. Cover and let rise until doubled, about 40 minutes.

Bake in a preheated 375° oven for approximately 45 minutes until the loaf sounds hollow when lightly tapped.

Turn the bread out of the pans and cool on a wire rack before slicing.

GRANDMAMA'S WHITE BREAD

Whole wheat flour was considered rather coarse in my grandmother's day, while white flour was obviously refined, literally and figuratively. Of coarse this won't win any nutrition awards, but the taste and texture are divine. Such a treat toasted and buttered for breakfast.

{ MAKES 2 MEDIUM LOAVES. }

2   cups milk
¼   cup butter
¼   cup shortening
3   cups plus 3 cups all-purpose flour
1   teaspoon salt
1   package dry yeast

Scald the milk and pour over the butter and shortening. Let cool to just warm. Mix 3 cups of flour, the salt, and yeast together in a large mixing bowl and pour the warm milk mixture over. Beat together for 3 minutes. Turn dough into a greased bowl, cover, and let rise until for about 1 hour and 30 minutes, until double.

Beat in the additional flour (if the dough seems too sticky add up to 1 cup more) and knead for 5 minutes. Again, place in a greased bowl and let rise for about 2 hours until doubled.

Divide and shape into 2 loaves, place in greased loaf pans, and let rise about 2 more hours until doubled.

Bake at 350° for 40 minutes, until nicely browned and the loaf sounds hollow when tapped. Turn out onto a wire rack to cool before slicing.

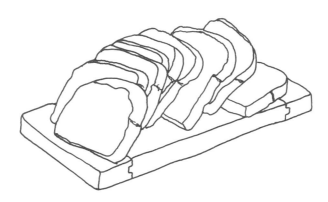

YEAST ROLLS

these almost melt in your mouth.

{ MAKES 24 ROLLS. }

1   cup whole milk
2   packages dry yeast
½   cup butter, melted
¼   teaspoon salt
¼   cup sugar
2   eggs
4½   to 5 cups all-purpose flour
     More melted butter

Warm the milk in a small saucepan over low heat. Mix ⅓ cup of the milk with the dry yeast in a small bowl and let sit until bubbly. In the bowl of an electric mixer combine the remaining milk, melted butter, salt, and sugar, and beat until the sugar is dissolved.

Add the beaten eggs and bubbly yeast.

Add the flour, ¼ cup at a time, beating on high speed. This step should take at least 5 minutes. When the dough gets too stiff to beat, stir in the rest of the flour by hand, if necessary, to make a soft dough. Turn out onto a floured surface and knead for 5 minutes, until smooth and satiny. Place the dough in greased bowl, turning to grease the top. Cover and let rise in a warm place until light and doubled in size. (I have also covered the dough well and placed it in the refrigerator overnight. This works really well.)

Punch down the dough and roll out on a floured surface to ½-inch thickness. Cut with a 3-inch round cookie cutter. Brush each roll with melted butter and fold in half to make half circles. Pinch the edge lightly to hold, so the rolls don't unfold as they rise. Place in 2 greased 13x9-inch pans, cover, and let rise again until double. (If you refrigerated the dough, this will take a little longer.)

Bake the rolls at 350° for 20 to 25 minutes or until golden brown. Remove from the pan immediately and brush with more melted butter. Don't use the same butter you used when forming the rolls, melt some fresh just for this step.

HOT CROSS BUNS

{ MAKES 24 BUNS. }

To modify the Yeast Roll recipe into hot cross buns, simply add ½ teaspoon more sugar and 1 teaspoon of cinnamon. Add 1 cup of currants with the flour. After the dough has risen for 1 hour, divide into 24 even pieces. Dip these into butter and flatten slightly as you press them onto a greased baking sheet. Use scissors or a sharp knife to snip a small cross in the top of each bun and let rise for 2 hours. Bake about 5 to 10 minutes longer than rolls. Remove from the oven and ice lightly with an icing made of confectioners' sugar, milk, and a bit of vanilla.

GINGER DATE NUT BREAD

{ MAKES 2 LOAVES. }

1½ cups boiling water
1½ cups cut up dates (1 package)
 1 egg
 1 cup sugar
 1 tablespoon melted butter
 ½ cup chopped crystallized ginger
2¾ cups all-purpose flour
 2 teaspoons baking soda
 ¼ teaspoon salt
 1 cup chopped walnuts
 1 teaspoon vanilla extract

Pour the water over the dates; allow to stand 20 minutes.

In a large bowl beat the egg; add the sugar and melted butter and beat well. Drain the water from the dates into the egg mixture. Sift the flour, soda, and salt into the mixture of egg and water. Stir until mixed Add the chopped nuts, dates, and vanilla. Pour into 2 9x5-inch loaf pans. Bake at 325° for 1 hour.

BANANA BREAD WITH BLACK WALNUTS

I love the flavor of black walnuts, which grow wild in the mid–South. Some people find them a little overpowering.
Substitute English walnuts, if you choose. The buttermilk makes this a moist and silky bread.

{ MAKES 1 LARGE LOAF. }

⅔   cup butter, softened
1⅓ cups sugar
2   eggs
3   to 4 bananas (1½ cups mashed banana)
3   cups all-purpose flour
1   teaspoon baking soda
1   teaspoon baking powder
⅓   cup buttermilk, clabber, or sour cream
1   teaspoon vanilla extract
1   cup choppedblack walnuts

Preheat the oven to 350°. Grease and flour 1 large or 2 small loaf pans. Cream the butter and the sugar and mix in the eggs, beating until light. Sift the dry ingredients and mix into the batter. Mix in the bananas and then the buttermilk, stirring just to blend. Fold in the walnuts and pour the batter into the prepared pan(s). Bake for 1 hour and 30 minutes for a large pan or 1 hour for the small.

STRAWBERRY BREAD

This is a nice gooey, sweet bread. Really great toasted.

[MAKES 2 LOAVES. }

1   cup butter
1½ cups sugar
    Grated zest and 1 teaspoon juice from 1 lemon
4   eggs
3   cups all-purpose flour
1   teaspoon salt
½   teaspoon baking soda
1   cup strawberry jam

1   cup chopped walnuts
½   cup sour cream

*P*reheat the oven to 325°. Grease and flour 2 medium loaf pans. Cream the butter with the sugar and lemon juice, beating until light. Add the eggs and beat well. Sift together the flour, salt, and soda, and mix in. Mix together the jam, nuts, and sour cream and fold into the batter. Pour the batter into the prepared loaf pans and bake for almost 1 hour, until a straw inserted in the center comes out clean. Cool in the pans for 10 minutes before turning out on wires to cool completely.

CRANBERRY LOAF

Tangy in flavor and truly beautiful. A lovely present.

{ MAKES 2 LOAVES. }

1   pound cranberries
2   cups all-purpose flour
2½ cups sugar
1   tablespoon baking powder
2   teaspoons salt
1   teaspoon baking soda
    Juice and zest from 2 oranges
    Juice and zest from 2 limes
2   eggs
¼   cup shortening
¼   cup water
2   cups chopped walnuts

*P*reheat the oven to 325°. Grease and flour 2 medium loaf pans. Rinse and dry the cranberries and roughly chop by hand. Sift together the dry ingredients in a medium bowl. Zest the oranges and limes before juicing. Measure the orange and lime juice to make 1 cup. Add more orange juice, if necessary. Beat the eggs in a large bowl. Melt the shortening and boil the water separately and mix these together with the juice. Pour the liquid into the eggs, beating. Add the dry ingredients, beating slowly until smooth. Fold in the cranberries, fruit zests, and walnuts. Fill the prepared loaf pans two-thirds full with the batter. Bake for 45 minutes, or until a straw inserted in the center comes out clean.

PUMPKIN BREAD

The buttermilk and pumpkin combine to give a satiny smooth texture to this bread.

{ MAKES 2 MEDIUM LOAVES. }

1½ cups sugar
⅔ cup shortening
4 eggs
2 cups puréed pumpkin
⅔ cup buttermilk
1 tablespoon bourbon
3½ cups all-purpose flour
½ teaspoon baking powder
2 teaspoons baking soda
2 teaspoons salt
2 teaspoons ground cinnamon
½ teaspoon grated nutmeg
1 cup chopped pecans

Preheat the oven to 350°. Grease and flour 2 medium loaf pans. Cream together the sugar and shortening in a large bowl. Beat in the egg until fluffy. Mix in the pumpkin, buttermilk, and bourbon. Sift together the dry ingredients and add to the batter, blending well. Fold in the nuts. Pour into the prepared pans. Bake for 1 hour until a straw inserted in the center comes out clean.

LEMON TEA BREAD

Delicate flavor and light texture. Just right with tea.

{ Makes 1 medium loaf. }

½   cup butter
1   cup sugar
2   eggs
1½   cups all-purpose flour
1   teaspoon baking powder
1   teaspoon salt
½   cup buttermilk
3   lemons, zested and juiced
½   cup ground almonds

Preheat the oven to 325°. Grease and flour a medium loaf pan. Cream the butter with the sugar. Add the eggs and beat until light. Sift the dry ingredients and mix in. Stir in the buttermilk, then the lemon juice and zest, and ground almonds. Pour the batter into the prepared pan. Bake for 50 minutes or until a straw inserted in the center comes out clean.

While the bread is baking, stir together the juice of 1 additional lemon with ½ cup of sugar. Remove the baked bread from the oven and use a straw or skewer to poke several holes in the top. Pour the lemon and sugar over and let the bread sit in the pan for at least 1 hour before removing.

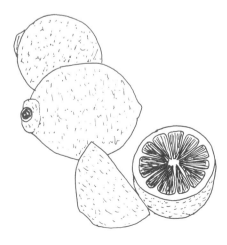

CHOCOLATE ICING

{ MAKES ICING FOR 1 TWO-LAYER OR SHEET CAKE. }

2	egg yolks
¼	cup milk, scalded
2¼	cups confectioners' sugar
1	tablespoon vanilla extract
2	ounces unsweetened chocolate
1	tablespoon butter

Beat the egg yolks. Add the milk, sugar, and vanilla. Beat well. Melt the chocolate with the butter in the top of a double boiler over simmering water. Pour the chocolate and butter into the egg mixture and mix. Let cool to spreading consistency.

GINGER CAKE

Such a comfort, ginger cake. It takes the chill right out of the air.

{ SERVES 4 TO 6. }

½   cup butter
½   cup sugar
½   cup dark molasses
 2   eggs, well beaten
½   cup milk
½   teaspoon salt
 1   teaspoon baking soda
 2   teaspoons ground ginger
2½   cups all-purpose flour

Preheat the oven to 350°. Cream the butter with the sugar. Beat in the molasses and then the eggs and milk. Sift together the dry ingredients and mix in well. Pour into a greased loaf pan and bake for 40 minutes, until a tester inserted in the center comes out clean.

Let cool slightly and turn out onto wire racks. Serve warm with whipped cream.

CARAMEL CAKE

*Around these parts a "caramel cake" is frequently a white cake with caramel icing. This cake is really caramel,
with real caramel in it. Don't be frightened. You can do this, and you'll love it.*

{ SERVES 8 TO 12. }

½   cup sugar
½   cup boiling water

½   cup butter
1½ cups sugar
 2 eggs, separated
 3 cups all-purpose flour
 2 teaspoons baking powder
 1 cup milk
 1 teaspoon vanilla extract

Place the sugar in a heavy saucepan over medium high heat and stir constantly until
it begins to melt and brown. Remove from the fire and pour in the boiling water, stirring
like crazy. Return to the the heat and stir until you have a thick syrup. Set aside.

Preheat the oven to 350°. Grease 2 9-inch cake pans with shortening and dust with
flour. Cream the butter with the sugar and beat in the egg yolks. Sift together the dry
ingredients and mix in alternating with the milk, in 2 additions. Add the vanilla extract
and 3 tablespoons of caramel and mix well. Beat the egg whites stiff and fold in. Pour
into the prepared cake pans and bake for about 30 minutes until a tester inserted
comes out clean.

Cool in the pans for several minutes, then turn out onto wire racks, and let cakes
cool completely. Ice with Boiled White Icing (recipe follows).

BOILED WHITE ICING

{ MAKES ICING FOR 1 TWO-LAYER CAKE. }

1   cup water
2   cups plus ¼ cup sugar
1   tablespoon light corn syrup
3   egg whites, at room temperature
1   teaspoon vanilla extract

Boil the water and pour in the 2 cups of sugar and corn syrup. Boil hard until it reaches soft ball stage (240°).

While the syrup is boiling, beat the whites foamy, sprinkle in ¼ cup of sugar, and beat until very stiff, almost dry. When the syrup reaches temperature, pour it into the side of the bowl of the egg whites in a thin steady stream, beating like mad until all of the syrup is incorporated.

SPICE CAKE

Really a spice cake, with even a subtle bit of cayenne. This is an old, old recipe.

{ SERVES 8 TO 12. }

1   cup butter
2   cups firmly packed brown sugar
7   egg yolks
1   egg
1   cup buttermilk
1   cup molasses
5   cups all-purpose flour
1   teaspoon baking soda
1   teaspoon ground cloves
2   teaspoons ground ginger
2   teaspoons ground cinnamon
1   teaspoon grated nutmeg
¼   teaspoon cayenne pepper

Preheat the oven to 350°. Grease 2 9-inch round cake pans. Cream together the butter and the sugar. Beat in the eggs, beating to a light batter. Mix in the buttermilk and molasses. Sift together the flour and soda and mix in. Finally, mix in all of the spices. Pour into the prepared cake pans and bake for about 30 minutes, until a tester inserted in the center comes out clean.

Let cool in the pans for 10 minutes. Turn out onto wire racks and cool completely. Put together and ice with Caramel Icing (recipe follows).

CARAMEL ICING

{ MAKES ICING FOR 1 TWO-LAYER CAKE. }

1   pound light brown sugar
3   tablespoons all-purpose flour
¾   cup cold water
½   cup butter
1   16-ounce box confectioners' sugar, sifted
1   teaspoon vanilla extract

Mix together the brown sugar, flour, water, and butter in a saucepan off the heat. Dissolve thoroughly and cook to about 236°, just under the soft ball stage. Remove from the heat and cool without stirring for 10 minutes.

Add the confectioners' sugar and vanilla and beat to a spreading consistency. If it gets too stiff, thin it with a little cream or milk.

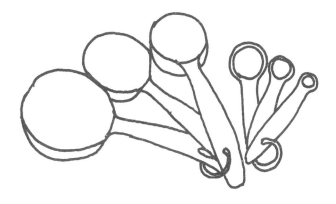

GRANDMAMA'S PINEAPPLE CAKE

Actually, a white cake with pineapple icing. This cake appeared on the cut glass cake stand for special occasions like birthdays. Grandmama liked to tie ribbon around coins and slide them under the cake for children to pull out. That way everyone got a favor.

{ SERVES 8 TO 12. }

½   cup shortening
1½ cups sugar
3   cups all-purpose flour
3   teaspoons baking powder
1   teaspoon salt
1   cup water
1   teaspoon vanilla extract
4   egg whites

Preheat the oven to 350°. Grease and flour 2 9-inch cake pans. Cream together the shortening and sugar. Sift the dry ingredients and add alternately with the water. Add the vanilla and beat thoroughly. Beat the egg whites stiff and fold into the batter. Pour into 2 greased 9-inch cake tins and bake for 20 minutes, until a tester inserted in the center comes out clean.

Let cool in the pans for 10 minutes before turning out onto racks and cooling entirely.

PINEAPPLE ICING

{ MAKES ICING FOR 1 TWO-LAYER CAKE. }

1   8¼-ounce can crushed pineapple
⅔   cup water
2   cups sugar
1   egg white
1   dozen marshmallows

Drain the pineapple very well, reserving the juice. While the cakes are cooling, pour the juice from the pineapple over both layers. Set the pineapple aside.

Boil the water and sugar together to 238° (soft ball). While that is cooking, beat the egg white stiff. Pour the syrup over the egg white in a thin stream, beating. Add the marshmallows and beat until cool. Fold in the well-drained pineapple. Spread the icing between the layers, on the sides, and over the top of the stacked cakes. If the icing is too runny, beat in confectioners' sugar until it thickens enough to cling to the cake.

BLACKBERRY JAM CAKE

A yummy old fashioned dessert. Slightly chewy and plenty sweet. Great with a cold, cold glass of milk.

{ SERVES 8 TO 12. }

1　cup butter

2　cups sugar

5　eggs, separated

1　cup buttermilk

4　cups all-purpose flour

2　teaspoons baking soda

2　teaspoons ground cinnamon

2　cups blackberry jam

　　Caramel Icing (see page 243)

Preheat the oven to 350°. Grease 2 9-inch cake pans with shortening and dust with flour. Set aside.

Cream the butter with the sugar. Beat in the egg yolks one at a time, and then the buttermilk. Sift together the flour, soda, and cinnamon, and mix in. Stir in the jam. Beat the egg whites stiff and fold in. Pour the batter into the prepared cake pans and bake for about 30 minutes, until a tester comes out clean. Spread with Caramel Icing.

CHOCOLATE ZUCCHINI CAKE

{ SERVES 12. }

2¼ cups sifted all-purpose flour
1 cup unsweetened cocoa powder
1½ teaspoons baking soda
2½ teaspoons baking powder
1 teaspoon cinnamon
1 teaspoon salt
1¾ cups sugar
¾ cup (1 stick) unsalted butter, room temperature
3 large eggs
1 teaspoon vanilla extract
½ cup buttermilk
2 cups grated unpeeled zucchini (about 2½ medium)

Preheat the oven to 325°. Butter and flour 2 9-inch round baking pans. Sift the flour, cocoa powder, baking soda, baking powder, cinnamon, and salt into a medium bowl.

In a large bowl beat the sugar, butter, and oil in large bowl until well blended. Add the eggs 1 at a time, beating well after each addition. Beat in the vanilla extract. Mix in the dry ingredients alternately with the buttermilk in 3 additions each. Mix in the grated zucchini. Pour the batter into the prepared pans.

Bake the cake for about 50 minutes, until a tester inserted into the center of the cake comes out clean. Cool the cake completely in the pan. Ice with Cream Cheese Cocoa Frosting.

CREAM CHEESE COCOA FROSTING

{ MAKES FROSTING FOR 1 TWO-LAYER CAKE. }

1 pound (2 packages) cream cheese, softened
½ cup cocoa
2 cups confectioners' sugar

In a medium bowl whisk all ingredients together. Store covered in the refrigerator for up to 1 week.

FUDGE CAKE

This is yummy, gooey, and chocolatey, and can be made in one pan in a matter of minutes.

{ MAKES ABOUT 12 SQUARES. }

½   cup butter
1   cup sugar
1½ squares chocolate
¾   cup all-purpose flour
¼   teaspoon salt
¼   teaspoon baking powder
2   eggs
1   teaspoon vanilla extract
1   cup broken walnuts

Preheat the oven to 325°. Grease and flour a 9-inch square baking pan.

Melt the butter, sugar, and chocolate together. Sift the flour, salt, and baking powder into this. Add the eggs, vanilla, and nuts. Mix well and pour into the prepared pan. Bake for 35 minutes.

Let cool completely. This is very rich and delicious as is. My mother likes to ice it with a dark chocolate frosting, sending the choco-meter way over the top.

STRAWBERRY SHORTCAKE

*This is, in my humble opinion, the best dessert ever created by anyone ever in the history of the world.
I believe it must be one of Mama's favorite's, too, because every year on at least one Sunday during the early
summer, Mama would serve our family of five an entire strawberry shortcake for lunch after Sunday school.
No veggies, no meat, just one fifth of a cake per person.*

As the high school dishwashers at work taught me to say, "Mom rocks." So does the cake.

{ SERVES 6 TO 8. }

2   quarts strawberries
½   cup sugar

1   pint heavy cream
3   tablespoons confectioners' sugar

2   cups all-purpose flour
4   teaspoons baking powder
1   teaspoon salt
2½   teaspoons firmly packed light brown sugar
⅓   cup shortening
⅔   cup buttermilk
1   tablespoon melted butter

Rinse, hull, and slice the strawberries, reserving about 12 good-looking ones for the
top of the cake. Place the sliced berries in a bowl and pour the sugar over. Stir well
and even mash a little. Set aside.

Whip the cream with the confectioners' sugar to hold soft peaks. Refrigerate while
you make the shortcake.

Preheat the oven to 425°. Sift together the flour, baking powder, salt, and brown
sugar. Use your fingertips to work in the shortening until the mixture resembles cornmeal. Add the buttermilk and butter, and mix to a soft dough. Roll out on a floured
board to 1/2-inch thickness. Use a 9-inch cake pan as a "cutter," making 2 circles.
Grease the inside of 2 cake pans and place the dough loosely inside. Bake for 30 or
so minutes, until cooked through. Turn out the shortcakes and place one on a serving
platter. Spread with butter. Spread about two-thirds of the macerated berries on top.
Place the other cake over this. Top with the remaining macerated berries and lightly
spread or spoon the whipped cream over. Top with the reserved whole berries and
serve immediately.

This gets a little sloppy, but that's half the fun. It's a luxurious kind of sloppiness.
Use this with any summer fruit: blackberries, plums, peaches, cherries, blueberries,

raspberries, and any combination thereof. Don't let the shortcake cool too much before serving. I love the warmth of the cake with the cool cream and refreshing berries.

ANGEL FOOD CAKE

A virtually fat-free dessert which, amazingly enough, tastes divine. I guess that's where they get the name.

{ SERVES 8 TO 12. }

1	cup all-purpose flour
½	cup confectioners' sugar
½	teaspoon salt
¾	cup superfine sugar
12	egg whites, at room temperature
1	teaspoon cream of tartar
1	teaspoon vanilla extract
1	teaspoon almond extract

Preheat the oven to 325°. Have ready an ungreased standard bundt pan. Sift the flour with the confectioners' sugar and salt. Set aside. Sift the superfine sugar and set aside.

Place the whites in a mixing bowl and use an electric mixer to beat the whites on low until frothy. Add the cream of tartar and continue beating. Gradually add the superfine sugar with the mixer running. Whip until almost stiff. The whites should have a high sheen. Fold in the almond and vanilla by hand with a whisk. Gradually fold in the flour mixture with a rubber spatula, just folding in and not over mixing. Be sure to scrape down to the bottom of the bowl as you go.

Pour the batter into the tube pan. Gently tap the pan on the work surface to release any air bubbles. Place in the center of the oven and bake for 45 minutes, until well risen and golden brown.

Remove from the oven and set upside down, inverted through the funnel onto a bottle. Let the cake sit that way until completely cooled, up to several hours.

Slice into large wedges and serve with fresh fruit and whipped cream, lemon curd, or raspberry sauce.

POUND CAKE

Oh my goodness, I do love pound cake. I sneak chunks of it and eat it plain. I toast pound cake and proclaim it breakfast. I add whipped cream and berries for a fancy dessert.

Pound cake is so-called because of the recipe, which calls for a pound of fat, a pound of sugar, and a pound flour. Easy to remember. Actually hard to forget. A thousand variations have been created upon the theme. This recipe is a very old-fashioned one with no leavening except for the eggs. It makes a simple, dense, and decadent cake.

{ SERVES 8 TO 12. }

1	pound butter
1	pound sugar
10	eggs, separated
2	tablespoons whiskey
1	teaspoon vanilla extract
1	pound all-purpose flour (4 cups)
½	teaspoon salt

Preheat the oven to 325°. Grease and lightly flour 2 medium loaf pans. Cream the butter well, add the sugar and cream until light and fluffy. Beat the egg yolks and mix in until very light. Stir in the whiskey and vanilla. Sift together the flour and salt and stir in. Beat the egg whites to soft peaks. Gently fold into the batter until just blended. Turn into the loaf pans and bake for 1 hour, or when the cake springs to the touch.

Cool in the pans for 10 minutes before turning out onto wire racks to cool thoroughly.

CORNMEAL POUND CAKE

The cornmeal gives this an interesting texture. I love it with whipped cream and fresh fruit in a simple syrup.

{ MAKES 2 CAKES, 8 SERVINGS EACH. }

1½ cups buttermilk

 1 cup cornmeal

3¼ cups all-purpose flour

 1 tablespoon baking powder

1½ teaspoons baking soda

¾ teaspoon salt

12 ounces (3 sticks) unsalted butter, at room temperature

1½ cups sugar

 3 eggs

In a medium bowl mix together the buttermilk and cornmeal; let soak for 45 minutes.

Preheat the oven to 350°. Butter and flour 2 8-inch tube cake pans.

In a medium bowl sift together the flour, baking powder, baking soda, and salt.

In a large bowl cream together the butter and sugar until fluffy. Add the eggs 1 at a time, beating well after each addition. Fold the cornmeal mixture and dry ingredients alternately into the creamed mixture. Divide the batter between prepared pans. Bake for about 40 minutes, or until a toothpick inserted into the cake comes out clean.

Let the cakes cool in the pan for 5 minutes before turning out onto a wire rack to cool.

FRUIT CAKE

He who dislikes fruitcake has never had my mother's, or at least never helped her make it. This was one of several cooking productions performed in our household just prior to Christmas, in which we all took part. My older sisters got to cut out the paper to line the pans, and I was assigned the task of greasing the paper. I eventually graduated to the stature of fruit chopper after my sisters had deserted us for other pursuits.

This is a very special gift to receive, delightful to nibble on with a spot of sherry on a bitter cold afternoon. The store–bought kind just misses the point, and the taste.

{ MAKES 7 ONE-POUND LOAVES, OR APPROXIMATELY 4 TUBE CAKES. }

1	pound white raisins
½	pound citron, chopped
½	pound candied cherries, chopped
½	pound candied pineapple, chopped
¼	pound orange peel
¼	pound lemon peel
½	cup sherry

1	cup butter
2	cups sugar
3½	cups all-purpose flour
3	teaspoons baking powder
½	teaspoon salt
1	cup milk
6	egg whites

1	cup coconut
½	pound almonds
½	pound pecans

Soak the chopped fruit in the sherry overnight.

Line baking pans (tube pans or loaves) with greased brown paper (we used grocery bags) or parchment. Preheat the oven to 325°.

Cream together the butter and sugar. Sift the dry ingredients together and add alternately with the milk. Beat the egg whites stiff and fold in. Stir in the coconut, almonds, pecans, and fruit.

Pour into the prepared pans and bake until a straw inserted in the center comes out clean. Pour the remaining sherry over while the cakes are still warm in the pans. Let the cakes cool in the pans before turning out.

BUTTERSCOTCH BROWNIES

Rich and very sweet—a good alternative to chocolate.

{ MAKES 8 SERVINGS. }

½   cup butter
1½ cups firmly packed brown sugar
 2 eggs
1½ cups self-rising flour
 1 teaspoon vanilla extract
 1 cup chopped pecans or walnuts

Preheat the oven to 350°. Grease a 9x13-inch pan. Melt butter in a saucepan. Add sugar and bring to a boil over low heat, stirring constantly. Remove from heat and let cool for ten minutes. Beat in the eggs, one at a time. Add the flour and vanilla and stir well. Fold in the nuts and pour into the prepared pan. Bake for 35 minutes. Let cool before cutting.

HELLO MOLLIES

This is my take on the classic "Hello Dolly."

{ MAKES 6 SERVINGS. }

½   cup butter, melted
1½ cups graham cracker crumbs
 1 cup chocolate chips
 1 cup sweetened coconut flakes
 1 14-ounce can sweetened condensed milk
½   cup peanuts

Preheat the oven to 350°. Pour the melted butter into a 9-inch square baking pan. Sprinkle the graham cracker crumbs over the butter and combine with a fork; press evenly into the bottom of the pan. Sprinkle chocolate chips evenly over the crust. Sprinkle coconut evenly over the chocolate; pour the sweetened condensed milk evenly over the coconut. Top with nuts. Bake for 25 to 30 minutes, until the middle is melted.
   Cool at least 20 minutes before cutting.

LEMON SQUARES

These are a dessert staple for boxes and buffets.

{ MAKES 8 SERVINGS. }

FOR THE CRUST:

1   cup all-purpose flour
¼   cup confectioners' sugar
½   cup butter

FOR THE FILLING:

    Juice and grated zest from 3 lemons
1   cup sugar
2   eggs, lightly beaten
2   tablespoons all-purpose flour

Preheat the oven to 350°. Mix together the flour and sugar. Cut the butter in bits and mix in just until the mixture will cling together. Press into the bottom of a 9-inch square pan and bake for 10 minutes, while you prepare the filling.

   Zest the lemons before you juice them. Beat the sugar into the eggs and stir in the other ingredients. Pour over the pre-baked bottom layer and cook for 20 minutes longer, until set.

DIVINITY FUDGE

Smooth and very, very sweet. A nice present for the holidays.

{ SERVES 6 TO 8. }

  2   egg whites
2½ cups sugar
 ½ cup light corn syrup
 ½ cup water
1½ cups chopped pecans
 ½ teaspoon vanilla extract

In a medium bowl beat the egg whites stiff. Set aside.

Mix the sugar, corn syrup, and water in a heavy saucepan. Cook on medium-high heat, stirring constantly, until the soft ball stage is reached. Test by putting 1 or 2 drops in cold water. This should hold a ball that will remain soft when rolled between your fingers. A candy thermometer should register 235°.

Pour half of the mixture over the stiff egg whites. Return the pan to the heat and continue cooking to the hard ball stage (250° on a candy thermometer).

Add the egg white mixture along with the nuts and vanilla and stir together. Spread onto a buttered dish. Cut the fudge before it completely sets.

PEANUT BUTTER FUDGE

Rich and silky.

{ SERVES 8. }

  3   cups sugar
  3   tablespoons light corn syrup
 ½ cup peanut butter
1¼ cups whole milk
  2   tablespoons butter
  2   teaspoons vanilla extract

Butter a 7x11-inch pan. In a large heavy saucepan combine the sugar, corn syrup, peanut butter, and milk. Stir well. Cook over medium heat to soft ball stage. Remove from the heat and add the peanut butter and vanilla. Beat until the mixture is thick and has lost its gloss. Pour into the prepared pan. Let cool and cut into squares.

CHOCOLATE FUDGE

A trio of fudge (chocolate, peanut butter, and divinity) makes a tasty old–fashioned Christmas gift.

{ SERVES 6 TO 8. }

2¾ cups sugar

4 ounces unsweetened chocolate

3 tablespoons butter, plus more for greasing pan

1 cup half-and-half

1 tablespoon corn syrup

1 tablespoon vanilla extract

1 cup chopped, roasted nuts, optional

Grease an 8-inch square pan with butter. In a heavy-bottomed saucepan combine the sugar, chocolate, 1½ tablespoons of the butter, half-and-half, and corn syrup. Heat over medium heat, stirring with a wooden spoon until the sugar is dissolved and the chocolate is melted. Increase the heat and bring to a boil. Reduce the heat to medium-low, cover, and boil for 3 minutes. Remove the cover and attach a candy thermometer to the pot. Cook until the thermometer reads 234°. Remove from the heat and add the remaining butter. Do not stir. Let the mixture cool for 10 minutes or until it drops to 130°. Add the vanilla and nuts, if desired, and mix until well-blended and the shiny texture becomes matte. Pour into the prepared pan. Let sit in a cool dry area until firm. Cut into 1-inch pieces and store in an airtight container for up to a week.

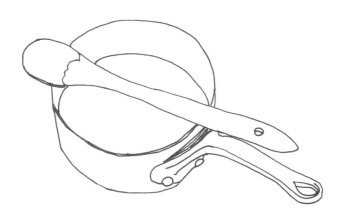

PEANUT BRITTLE

This is easy and makes a great holiday present.

{ SERVES 6 TO 8. }

1½ cups sugar

½ cup light corn syrup

¼ teaspoon salt

3 tablespoons cold water

2 cups raw shelled peanuts

1 teaspoon baking soda

Grease a cookie sheet with shortening. Set aside.

Combine all of the ingredients except the peanuts in a heavy 1-quart saucepan and bring to a rolling boil. Pour in the peanuts. Keep at a rolling boil and stir the peanuts until they begin to pop and the syrup is a golden amber. Remove from the stove and stir in the soda. Beat until well mixed. Pour onto the prepared cookie sheet and let cool. Break into pieces.

CARAMEL APPLES

Surprise! I use the easy way! It happens to be the best.

{ SERVES 12. }

3 pounds caramel candies

½ cup evaporated milk

12 super-crisp apples

Place the candies and milk in a deep saucepan and melt over low heat, stirring occasionally, until melted and creamy.

While those are heating, rinse the apples and use wooden sucker sticks to pierce through the core of each apple.

Stand each apple in the pan with the caramel and spoon the caramel over the apple.

Rest the caramel apples on wax paper and chill to harden the caramel.

POPCORN BALLS

A Halloween necessity. Mama had us helping her to make these as little, little girls. She always buttered our hands to coat us against the hot candy. We realized that we were performing a dangerous but vital duty and took our jobs very seriously.

{ MAKES ABOUT 24 BALLS. }

6   quarts popped corn
2   cups sugar
1½ cups water
½   teaspoon salt
½   cup light corn syrup
1   teaspoon vinegar
1   teaspoon vanilla extract

Shake the popped corn in a bowl and remove any unpopped kernels that could prove hazardous to the teeth.

Combine the sugar, water, salt, corn syrup, vinegar, and vanilla in a saucepan. Bring to a boil and cook to the hard ball stage (250°). Pour the sugar mixture over the corn and stir. Butter your hands to press the mixture into balls while still hot. Be careful, and remember it is hot.

ORANGE CANDIED PECANS

Sweet? Savory? Well, a little of both. Great with cocktails, or to finish a grand meal.

{ SERVES 6 TO 8. }

Grated zest and juice from 4 oranges
2   cups sugar
2   pounds pecan halves
½   teaspoon salt
¼   teaspoon cayenne pepper
1   teaspoon ground cinnamon

Grate the zest from the oranges and then juice. Pour into a nonreactive saucepan along with the sugar and cook to 240°, the soft ball stage. Place the pecan halves in a bowl and sprinkle the salt, cayenne, and cinnamon over. Pour the candy over this and stir. Turn onto a cookie sheet and let cool. Break apart when cool enough to handle.

PRALINES

This is a softer praline than most folks are used to. They melt in your mouth.

{ MAKES ABOUT 2 DOZEN. }

2½ cups sugar
 1 cup milk
 3 tablespoons butter
    Vanilla extract
 1 cup nuts

Boil a scant 2 cups sugar with the milk. Melt the rest of the sugar in a heavy saucepan on top of the stove, stirring to avoid burning. When it begins to boil, pour in the milk and sugars. Cook, stirring, until it forms a ball. Add the butter, vanilla, and nuts, mixing well. Drop by spoonfuls onto waxed paper and allow to cool.

GINGERSNAPS

A good chewy gingersnap and cold glass of milk makes a great after-school treat. Good for grown-ups, too!

{ MAKES ABOUT 4 DOZEN COOKIES. }

 ¾ cup butter
 1 cup sugar
 1 egg
 ¼ cup molasses
 2 cups all-purpose flour
 1 tablespoon ground ginger
 1 teaspoon cinnamon
 ½ teaspoon salt
 ½ teaspoon baking soda
    Sugar

In a large bowl cream the butter and 1 cup of sugar until light. Add the egg and molasses; beat well. In a separate bowl combine the flour, spices, salt, and soda. Add the dry ingredients to the creamed mixture, blending well. Shape into small balls and roll in sugar. Bake at 325° for 12 to 15 minutes.

TOLL HOUSE COOKIES

A crispy chocolate chip cookie. Grandmother considered the chewy version "raw."
This, she assured me, was a chocolate chip cookie to be proud of.

{ MAKES ABOUT 3 DOZEN COOKIES. }

1   cup butter
¾   cup sugar
¾   cup firmly packed dark brown sugar
2   eggs
2¼ cups all-purpose flour
1   teaspoon baking soda
½   teaspoon salt
1   teaspoon vanilla extract
2½ teaspoons water
1   12-ounce package chocolate chips

Cream the butter with the sugars and beat in the eggs. Sift together the flour, soda, and salt, and add to the sugar mixture. Mix thoroughly. Add the vanilla and water and mix thoroughly. Stir in the chocolate chips. Refrigerate for about 30 minutes.

Preheat the oven to 350°. Drop the mixture by teaspoonfuls onto a greased cookie sheet and bake for about 10 minutes. They are best slightly undercooked. Let cool on the baking sheet before trying to remove.

MACAROONS

These are used in lots of frozen and congealed desserts and are wonderful on their own, as well.

[MAKES ABOUT 28 COOKIES. }

1   8-ounce can almond paste
1   cup sugar
3   unbeaten egg whites
¼   cup all-purpose flour
¼   cup confectioners' sugar

Preheat the oven to 350°. Work the almond paste and sugar together. Add egg whites. Sift together the flour and confectioners' sugar into the mix. Beat until smooth. Drop by spoonfuls onto a cookie sheet covered with parchment paper. Bake for 15 to 18 minutes, until light brown.

MARY MELL CLEMENTS' SUGAR COOKIES

I found this recipe in my grandmother's notes. My mother tells me that Mary Mell is alive and well and a member of her study group. She just turned ninety.

I like to sprinkle the tops of these with granulated sugar and almond pieces.

{ MAKES ABOUT 4 DOZEN COOKIES. }

1   cup sugar
1   cup butter
2   eggs
2¼ cups all-purpose flour
1   teaspoon almond extract

Cream the sugar with the butter and beat in the eggs. Mix in the flour and almond extract. Mix thoroughly and chill before baking.

Preheat the oven to 350°. The dough may be rolled and cut out or formed into a log and sliced in ¼-inch circles. Bake on ungreased cookie sheet for 10 minutes, until the edges begin to brown. If you are topping with almonds, be careful that they don't get too brown—they can burn before you know it.

CRESCENT COOKIES

These are lovely, not too sweet cookies. Yummy with a cup of tea in the afternoon.

{ MAKES ABOUT 6 DOZEN COOKIES. }

½   cup butter
½   cup confectioners' sugar
2   teaspoons vanilla extract
2   cups all-purpose flour
1   cup finely chopped walnuts
    Additional confectioners' sugar

Preheat the oven to 350°. Cream the butter and sugar and mix in the vanilla. Add the flour and walnuts and mix thoroughly. The dough will be very stiff. Shape by hand into crescents. Place on ungreased cookie sheet and bake for about 30 minutes.

Roll in confectioners' sugar while they are still warm.

HERMITS

My grandmother's favorite cookie, chewy and full of spice. I found this recipe written down in a dozen places throughout her notes, always exactly the same. I think that she was trying to memorize it when her eyesight was failing.

{ MAKES ABOUT 3 DOZEN COOKIES. }

1 cup butter
1½ cups brown sugar
3 eggs
1 teaspoon baking soda
⅓ cup hot water
2 cups all-purpose flour
1 teaspoon ground cinnamon
½ teaspoon ground cloves
½ teaspoon ground allspice
½ teaspoon ground nutmeg
1 teaspoon salt
2 cups nuts
1 cup raisins

Preheat the oven to 350°. Grease a baking pan.

Cream together the butter and sugar. Beat in the eggs. Dissolve the soda in the hot water and stir in. Sift together the flour with the spices and salt and mix in, along with the nuts and raisins. Drop from a spoon onto the greased pan and bake for 15 minutes.

SNICKERDOODLES

These cookies make me smile just saying their name. All cookies smell good baking, but the aroma of cinnamon in Snickerdoodles could bring me inside on the sunniest day. Mama sent these to me at camp, in college, and even to culinary school in New York. I hid them under my bed and very rarely shared.

{ MAKES ABOUT 4 DOZEN COOKIES. }

1½ cups sugar
2 eggs
½ cup shortening

½　cup butter, softened

2¾　cups all-purpose flour

2　teaspoons cream of tartar

1　teaspoon baking soda

¼　teaspoon salt

2　tablespoons sugar

2　teaspoons ground cinnamon

℘reheat the oven to 400°. Cream together 1½ cups of sugar and the eggs with shortening and butter. Sift the dry ingredients and mix in. Mix 2 tablespoons of sugar and the cinnamon together. Form small balls of the dough and roll in the cinnamon and sugar. Place on lightly greased cookie sheet and press down slightly. Bake for 10 minutes.

PEANUT BUTTER COOKIES

This is based on Betty Crocker's classic cookie. Who doesn't crave these?!

{ MAKES ABOUT 2 DOZEN COOKIES. }

½　cup granulated sugar

½　cup packed brown sugar

½　cup peanut butter

½　cup (1 stick) butter, softened

1　egg

1¼　cups all-purpose flour

¾　teaspoon baking soda

½　teaspoon baking powder

¼　teaspoon salt

℘reheat the oven to 375°.

In a medium bowl mix the sugars, peanut butter, butter, and egg. Stir in the remaining ingredients. Cover and refrigerate about 2 hours or until firm.

Shape the dough into 1¼-inch balls. Place about 3 inches apart on an ungreased cookie sheet. Flatten in a crisscross pattern with a fork dipped into sugar.

Bake for 9 to 10 minutes or until light golden brown. Cool 5 minutes; remove the from cookie sheet. Cool on a wire rack.

TEA CAKES

These are the cookie that we always used for decorating and icing, but they are also tasty made simply with no topping. Grandmother almost always had a tin of tea cakes in the pantry, or at least a log of dough in the ice box waiting to be made up.

To make these a little different, substitute rose or orange water for the vanilla.

{ MAKES ABOUT 4 DOZEN COOKIES. }

1   cup butter
1   cup sugar
2   eggs
2   teaspoons baking soda
2   tablespoons milk
2   teaspoons vanilla extract
2   teaspoons cream of tartar
3½ cups all-purpose flour
    Pinch salt

Cream the butter and sugar, and mix in the eggs. Dissolve the baking soda in the milk and add, along with the vanilla. Sift the dry ingredients together and stir in. Mix thoroughly. If you are going to roll and cut out cookies, gather the dough into a ball and wrap in plastic wrap. Alternately, roll the dough into a log and wrap in waxed paper. In either form, chill the dough for 15 minutes before proceeding. This makes the dough easier to handle.

Preheat the oven to 300°. Either slice ¼-inch circles from the log or roll out the ball of dough to ¼-inch thickness on a floured surface and cut out in desired shapes. Bake the tea cakes for about 20 minutes until golden brown. Any leftover dough will keep refrigerated for several days.

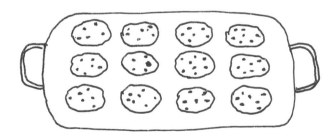